Published by D' Rose L.L.C.

Printed in the United States of America

ISBN: 978-0-9764819-6-6

House Hauntings and Negative Attachments

A Practitioner's Guide to Healing and Crossing Over Negative Spirits or Entities to the Higher Spiritual Planes

Disclaimer:

The book provides information from the author's point of view. It is not a diagnostic tool for medical or psychological diagnosis or treatment. It is recommended that an individual seek a licensed professional for all medical and or psychological treatment, for all ailments.

Table of Contents

Chapter One

Overview

Everything I share is from my experiences over the past 50 years. It has taken time to figure out and understand just a portion of the spiritual planes or levels. As a healer and teacher, my conscious interaction with the spirit plane is almost daily, and over the years, my relationship with these dimensions has blossomed with understanding.

This book is designed to help healing energy practitioners understand the astral planes and the spirits that dwell there. This is not a religious book, nor does it discuss exorcism practices. There are religious references, such as God, angels and so on, but this is a non-denominational text.

My background leads me to this type of work. I didn't seek it out, and I wouldn't recommend it as part of a practice unless a practitioner had a strong calling towards working with and crossing over negative spirits, also known as entities. Everyone is Divine bright light and therefore, capable of this kind of healing work. There are many practitioners all around the world that have their own methods and practices to clear negative energy from people or from places. These concepts are well established.

Humanity generates negative energy and a few individuals generate so much negative energy from causing harm to others that a piece of their spirit splits off from the whole and creates an entity. The main reason for this is an extreme disharmony in the spirit's polarity, which at its core is Divine. Entities sometimes take on a threatening image to be frightening, but what they really look like is balls of energy comprising of the negative energy that generated them.

The spiritual world doesn't use verbal communication. Spirits and Angels use telepathic communication. The human brain has to translate the telepathic communication it receives, which consists of intelligent intention, emotional motivation, and images. Therefore, a negative spirit or entity can take on any appearance and project that image to a person's mind, or the mind can create within its self an image that best represents the energy it's picking up on from the spirit. The image that a person's mind chooses is based on his or her belief system and memories. The image may or may not be accurate. Often, because entities trigger fear, the image is inaccurate most of the time. Please keep that in mind while reading this book.

My first memory of the spirit world took place when I was a very young child, around three or four years old. I remembered being bothered at night by a spirit that would touch my feet and back. Interesting enough, my brother, four years my senior, remembers being bothered by the same spirit as well even though we did not share our experiences with each other until decades later.

I also remember my parents fighting a lot over everything. They divorced each other while living in that home. We know negative spirits or entities amplify negative emotion, creating more anger and pain, causing an individual to feel overwhelmed by the emotion and losing perspective. This situation, of course, can be very difficult for a young couple, and I believe the negative energy in the house contributed to my parent's conflict.

The spiritual world within and around us is a fascinating and mysterious part of life. To start, I will answer commonly asked questions about the esoteric elements of life, and then explore entities, spirits, attachments, hauntings, and clearings.

Angels–Overseers of Life Path

At our core, we are the same as the angels: we come from the same Divine life force as all beings. Angels are beings that usually haven't incarnated into physical form. I am using the term 'angel' loosely for lack of a better identifiable term for these magnificent beings of light that project themselves as angels for our benefit. They express themselves on the various levels and realities of the cosmos. However, angels can incarnate, and they can spontaneously take on physical form if necessary.

Angels have the power to intervene for protection and assistance, so always ask for their help. They might not prevent a painful event from happening to you, but they will help you face the challenge. They will help you learn, grow, and heal from life's experiences.

In the beginning of my spiritual exploration, I found it doubtful that each person had a group of angels helping them day-to-day. It seemed too good to be true. I would think, "My life is not exciting, aren't they bored?" Later, as my understanding grew, I experienced profound moments of love and divine intervention and came to realize that my experience of reality and time is not the same for angels, spirit guides, and other beings.

I've discovered my angels were always there for me. They knew, before I did, when I needed them and, gratefully, I have had the privilege of physically seeing my angels besides strongly feeling their presence more times than I can count. These days, we talk almost daily, and they help me solve every problem under the sun.

They are spectacular; there is not a problem too small if it is important to you.
Their capacity to love and accept seems unbelievable, but they are genuine and powerful beings. Angels love you in the way you need it, and they always tell the truth. They empower the individual to think for him or herself and come to his or her own conclusions, even if wrong. An angel does not argue, and they accept your level of development without pressure or judgment. They trust you to grow and, eventually, to figure everything out. They trust you, and you should trust them.

Spirit Guides–Specialists

Most spirit guides have experienced numerous lifetimes, and they have intimate knowledge of the ego, shadow side, fear, and survival in physical form. Their perspective is relatable, and they usually specialize in certain skill sets that can assist you at different times. Spirit guides come and go, depending on what you need. A person can have several guides in one lifetime, and he or she may or may not know them from the current lifetime: an example would be a loved one that died. Our loved ones can become our spirit guide, or even a loved one from a different lifetime can also be a guide. Like angels, spirit guides usually have more than one charge, so they keep busy.

Soul–You

A soul is an angelic-like being that has incarnated into human form several times. It is you and me. We have a soul, and our soul contains within itself the different lifetimes we have experienced. Each lifetime has an individual identity called a spirit. Therefore, the soul contains all the unique spirits you have been. The soul is the gift of self, individuality, and free-will from the Divine.

Spirits–Many Different Kinds

When we are in body, our ego-self or individual identity refers to our spirit. When we die, our spirit returns to the soul-plane almost immediately, and we transition into our full selves. Some spirits do not make this transition because of personal issues such as extreme hatred or pain, and they are caught between dimensions on the astral plane, which are lower in vibration than the soul-planes. Some refer to them as ghosts. They create their own existence on the astral planes. Often, they will stay there, and then they gradually move up to the higher planes as time passes and as they observe and learn. Some refuse to change, but eventually someone in physical form or a guide in spirit form that does that kind of work assists the lost spirit. The ghost or spirit is harmless and does not intend to harm.

Entities

Entities are spirits that intend to interfere with the well-being and happiness of others. They feed off of fear and pain by amplifying negativity such as hate or blame. As a result, the people most vulnerable to entity attachments have extreme negative relationship issues with co-workers, family, and intimate partners; they often lack social and professional skills and emotional wisdom. Addicts are vulnerable to entities attaching energetically to them. (Note: attachment is 'not' possession. Attachment describes a connection or link). Entities do not want to transition into higher planes, nor do they care about anything other than themselves.

They identify with extreme hate and fear, which creates a delusional reality for them. You cannot reason with them, and it is best to cross them over to the higher planes with little interaction. If they focus on one person, they will form an attachment to that person, subconsciously trying to increase the individual's fear and/or anger. Remember, entities are balls of negative energy split off from the spirit/soul, therefore, their consciousness is limited.

Life after Death

Each of us has experienced the death and birth process many times over, and most of us have had no problems because we haven't generated extreme negative energy during our lifetime. The death process is the transition of the different levels of consciousness into the higher-planes or integration back into the soul. The last level of consciousness to make this transition is the body's survival function. Since it is the last to go, it can take the longest while the other levels of the spirit have already left. It is why you see people on their deathbed hanging on for days at a time. You know that most of the spirit has left, but the body is still alive. It takes time for the survival level of consciousness to fully let go. It resists the death process and prolongs the lifespan as long as possible, which is its purpose.

After all levels of consciousness have let go of the physical body, the spirit travels to a transitionary plane, eventually moving up into the soul-planes. There are many of these planes, and the evolution of the soul determines the desired soul-plane upon death. Like a magnet a spirit is pulled by his or her divine soul essence. Regardless of the level, the plane is welcoming, beautiful and relates to the individual's belief system. If you believe in Jesus, then you may see him. If you believe in the Buddha, then you will see him, and so on. During this time, the person relaxes, heals, and experiences his or her life review. God or the Divine doesn't orchestrate the life review process. Nobody is judging an individual after he or she transitions through the death process. The life review is for the individual spirit to look at his or her life journey for self-awareness and empowerment. A person not only gains understanding about the choices he or she chose, but also attains insight into the other choices and possibilities not chosen. This is a very interesting process. There is no judgement from a Divine source. Each soul, as pieces of the Divine, makes its own assessment of self.

After the personality/spirit has made his or her transition, options are available. You may decide to rest, learn on the different planes, socialize, merge with Divine essence, exist on one of the various planes or realities, become a spirit guide or reincarnate on one of the available planets. We are eternal beings. We don't have to do anything or reincarnate if we don't want to. Still, are we going to live one lifetime and then twiddle our thumbs for eternity in some spiritual realm? This concept makes little sense. After all, we are self-aware, intelligent, feeling beings. As an eternal being, I would rather experience my existence instead of simply observing it. Each spirit has one lifetime. This combination of DNA and experiences is unique and will never happen again, but as an infinite soul, you can experience many things.

The soul is always a version of itself. You carry the same gifts and knowledge with you from lifetime to lifetime, but there are endless possibilities of manifestation. For example, I am a student and a teacher everywhere I go. In this lifetime, I teach spirituality, healing, metaphysics, and so on. In previous lifetimes, I mastered martial arts, herbal medicine, and in another, I was a monk, to name a few. My core vibration of teaching is always with me, and your gifts are always with you from lifetime to lifetime. Of course, you can learn as many new skill-sets as you want, but there will always be those natural gifts that effortlessly flow from you.

The most important skill a soul learns is love. Learning about love and being in relationships with others is challenging. Whether or not we are in body, love is the common theme of learning: to give of self, to receive life's joy, to understand the truest forms of love, and to embody love is life's greatest gift.

Transforming fear and karma also has its difficulties. The possibilities for growth and creativity are endless. When you die, an entire universe opens up to you, and the decisions you make will start another cycle of adventure. The old saying that death is an ending and a beginning is true, so choose wisely. Whatever you begin, you will follow to completion.

I wrote this section to address some of the most common questions about the metaphysical world, but I encourage each person to make up his or her own mind. The information given here is just the tip of the iceberg. I encourage you to explore and to develop strong relationships with your angels and guides. They love you, and they have so much to offer.

Meditation is helpful, but it is not the only way to communicate with the Divine. Often, spending time with self, while enjoying a relaxing activity, provides an opportunity to communicate with the higher-self, Divine, angels, and guides. Connection while working is also available. When you are having a good day, and the energy is flowing, you are receptive to inspiration from the Divine.

Your spirituality (soul/divine-self: seventh chakra) and your daily life (spirit/ego-self: first chakra) are both life-force energy, and they work together creating your reality. It is important to at least have an elementary understanding of the cosmic world around us and, in doing so, we increase our wisdom and effectiveness in this world, for knowledge brings empowerment.

Angels, spirit guides, souls, spirits, entities and life after death are the topics we will cover. All the information I will share with you comes from my personal experiences and knowledge. May this book serve and empower your journey. Enjoy!

Chapter Two

Entity Basics

Entities are the primary focus of this book. For many years, people have repeatedly asked me to write a book about entities because many have encountered them during their lifetime. These experiences generally pass by with no long-term, negative consequences, but it's not uncommon for an entity to form an attachment to a person under the right conditions. Still, many people will go their whole lives without encountering a negative spirit or entity. I intended this book for those who don't have the same luck.

Entities are pieces of a spirit, but not all spirits are entities. Entities intentionally create harm while spirits, sometimes referred to as ghosts, are simply lost, confused, afraid, or in emotional pain.

What are entities? They are pieces of the spirit and or soul that stay attached to the Earth dimension when their consciousness and aura leave the physical body. This attachment prevents them from completely crossing over to the Soul plane/level, and they stay earth bound.

Why are they Earthbound? Powerful emotions like fear, hate, anger, and trauma induced emotions create a disharmony or split from the Divine energy within their soul, causing them to stay in the lower vibrations of the astral plane. While alive, in body, they had personal power issues and some enjoy inflicting harm on others.

What is the astral plane? It is a multi-level dimension bridging the Earth plane and the Soul planes. The level of positive and negative energies experienced can be vast, resulting in low vibrations that are dark and heavy, and also high vibrations that are lovely and light.

How many distinct entities are there? There are many. They can take on any form, including animals or someone you know, since they are no longer limited by a physical body. Some are angry and aggressive. There are some who are master manipulators. Some are confused, and some are manifestations of humanity's negativity, but humans generate all entities. I have come across many entities on the astral plane, and all of them are linked with humankind.

What can they do? They can attach to humans, houses, land, places, objects, and to a reality or moment in time. Again, I want to remind everyone, attachment is 'not' possession. They can drain your energy, manipulate and influence your thoughts, read your intentions and memories, give you bad dreams, use your anger and fears against you, amplify your emotion, move objects, cause pain, attack your astral body when sleeping, and influence the environment. Ultimately, they can make your life miserable and have a negative impact on your relationships.

Who is most vulnerable to attachment? Sensitive and empathic people can sense energy and that attracts entities, but just because a person is intuitive, doesn't automatically make him or her an entity magnet. People struggling with addiction are easy targets. Strong emotion like grief, hate, or anger attracts them. Chronic or long-term physical illness weakens the aura and creates an opportunity for entities. Hospitals are hot spots as well as funeral homes, places of trauma, houses built on lay-lines that cross or intersect, counselor offices, hotels, and, ironically, cruise ships. People that have a victimhood and or co-dependent consciousness are vulnerable because they have personal power issues. People that hate others are more likely to attract entities. Children are vulnerable from birth to seven and during puberty because of natural changes in the aura. Again, I want to remind everyone that it takes just the right combination of circumstances for an entity to attach to someone, and most people will never experience an entity attachment.

Are entities the same as Demons? When I was young, I thought all entities were demons. Some looked like the traditional description or image of demons: red eyes, pointy teeth, horns, etc. I have discovered two things in my work: everything I have encountered on the astral plane is generated by humans, and all entities clear or cross over to the Soul plane exactly the same way, regardless of what they look like.

I am not an expert, and the spirit world is complex and mysterious, so I cannot say I know all the answers. With time and experience, a practitioner gradually gains clarity and hopefully, understanding.

I can only go by my experience of what I have witnessed and what works. So far, it's my understanding that entities and demons are in the same classification or even perhaps the same being.

In my experience, humans generate the negative energy on the lower levels of the astral plane. If there are demons, and if some deity creates them, such as the Devil, they cross over to the Soul plane or to the light like any other lost entity or spirit. Due to a lack of knowledge, entities could be mistakenly labeled as demons. I have crossed over demon-like beings in my time, and they express themselves just like any other negative human I have encountered: filled with hate, anger, pain, aggression, and fear. Seems like a negative part of humanity to me, therefore, no actual measurable difference between the two, if any.

Chapter Three

My First Haunting

I was five going on six when I experienced my first vivid and intense haunting. It was so clear I can recall every detail to this day, and it scared me to death! Prior to this experience, I heard voices, felt the air chill; felt someone touching me or calling my name, but saw moving shadows only.

We lived in a very tiny house in White Cloud, Michigan during the late-1970's. When I played outside, I felt the creepy crawlies anytime I drifted close to the neighboring house, so I avoided it as much as possible. Still, the houses were built close together, making it impossible for me to keep my distance all the time.

During the day, I felt watched, but saw nothing. I also remember a continuous feeling of discomfort. I couldn't pin-point a specific reason, and as a child, I really didn't understand what I was feeling. My awareness was instinctual; I just knew something was wrong without understanding what generated the feeling.

It was the middle of the night, and a scratching sound awoke me. I looked up toward the sound and that is when I saw it outside my bedroom window, scratching its long, spiky fingernail down the glass. The entity was floating above the ground with smoky fog surrounding it. It had jet black hair, combed back from a gaunt, grey face, black shiny eyes, and sharp teeth. It smiled at me. (Again, as a reminder, this scary image was a projection from the entity to my child mind and not what it really looked like, which is a ball of negative energy).

I pulled the covers over my head, praying to God that I didn't see what I just saw. Carefully, pulling the covers down, I peeked over my blanket, and to my horror, it was still there. I panicked, and then something wonderful happened: a woman in a pink dress with light blondish brown hair appeared next to my bed. She got in the bed with me and put her arm around my shoulders.

She didn't speak with her voice, but I heard her voice in my head whisper, "He cannot enter." Instinctively, I knew two things: she was telling the truth, and she was my guardian angel. It was the first time I met her. I was not aware of her presence before that moment, nor did I know anything about guardian angels. I just knew she was safe, loving, and was there to protect me.

The entity continued to float outside of the bedroom window for a little longer. Nobody said a word, and eventually, with one last smirk, it left. My angel stayed until I fell asleep. I could sleep because she made me feel safer than I had ever felt before. When I woke, she was gone. I didn't see her again for several years.

I should actually thank that entity. Because of it, I started asking questions, and I wanted to learn everything I could about religion and the spiritual world after that experience. I started going to church by myself that same year. Essentially, it was an entity that inspired my path to become a healer and teacher.

I told my Mom the next day what happened, but she didn't know how to help me. Fortunately, we didn't have to live in that house for very long. We moved to a trailer, and for a few years my life was free of entity activity. Then, we moved to another home on seven acres. Both ghosts and entities haunted the land. I was around eight years old. This is when the trouble really started, and imagine my brutal disappointment when my guardian angel didn't show up to rescue me.

Years later, I went back in time and cleared the entity that floated outside my bedroom window in the middle of the night. There is no such thing as linear time in the spirit world. A little trick I have learned is the ability to go back a minute, an hour, day, week, or even several years to the original moment of visitation. I didn't know how to clear and cross over that entity at five years old, but I did when I was forty-five. I knew how thanks to my guardian angel taking a back seat and forcing me to learn how to work with entities for my well-being and, eventually, for the benefit of others in my healing work. There is no better motivation than emotional and mental survival.

My journey has been painful, frustrating, terrifying, magical, and extremely difficult. Let me clarify here, the Divine, angels, etc. did not abandon me, but they did, shall I say, give me plenty of opportunity to learn how to navigate and work with the spiritual world. They are my teachers, guides, and protectors, and I was their very reluctant, initially resentful student. I didn't want entities to be part of my life when I started this journey, and in the beginning I was bitter about it, but time moves on, and I accepted the path before me. In the following, I will share some of my more intense spiritual encounters, healings, and cross-overs. Notice, I didn't say banishments. Banishing a spirit from a location or person does not permanently resolve the situation. So, the old method of banishing entities/spirits back to a hell-like spiritual plane of existence serves no greater purpose: nothing is healed or resolved. Genuine progress is created through the healing process of crossing entities/spirits over to the soul-planes.

Healing practitioners are the most skilled at the job. The vibrations they generate are powerful enough to travel to the soul-planes, the healing energies they channel have the power to convert negative energy, and rigid beliefs, which are usually rooted in fear and judgment, do not restrict healers. However, if someone has proper comprehension, they can disperse negative energy without being trained as a healer.

Chapter Four

The Beginning of My Training

Previously, I stated how I went to church at a very young age by myself. I was seeking help, answers, and understanding of my haunting experiences. We moved a lot when I was young, so I had the privilege of attending a variety of churches. The people were kind to me, but ultimately, none could help me. I developed a wonderful relationship with the Divine, Jesus, and angels, however, because of my years with the church.

I continued to be involved with the church for a long time. After many years, I had a life-changing conversation with the youth pastor about a spirit that was haunting a church I attended.

On the weekends, after church services, I would stay behind and clean the church. As I was cleaning, I felt a presence or spirit follow me throughout the church. The spirit was invasive, negative, continuously crowding my personal space.

I tried to ignore its negativity, but eventually I brought my concerns to the pastor.

I asked him if he ever felt a spirit in the church. He said that he did, when he was alone, and that it made him feel uncomfortable. I asked if he knew what it was, and he said no. We discussed the spirit further, but he didn't know what it was, so he ignored it rather than seeking understanding. At that moment, I realized he didn't have the wisdom to guide me.

Over the next few years, I tried to understand the spiritual world, but my belief system lacked insight and wisdom. As a young person, I lacked experience and the knowledge that comes with it. I struggled for several years, but in my effort to understand, I attended intuitive classes and developed a meditation practice.

Learning how to meditate extensively has been one of the best decisions I have made in my life and I highly recommend it as a fundamental life skill for everyone, even if it isn't used for spiritual communication, but rather for well-being only. I developed an essential relationship with my angels, spirit guides, and animal totems. Without their guidance, patience, and protection, my spiritual skills would not be what they are today.

I studied physics, metaphysics, spirituality, meditation techniques, theology, psychology, and healing modalities. I fell in love with the field and became a healing practitioner and eventually a teacher as well. Still, nothing helped me resolve the entity issues.

The entities harassed me mostly at night, but I also had encounters during the day. Gradually, the encounters increased in intensity and frequency. At about that same time, my husband and I opened a healing center and metaphysical store. We were working long hours with little time off, and I couldn't get a decent night's sleep. Instead of being a time of serenity, nighttime had become filled with dread and worry.

I needed help, but there was no one around me that specialized in entities and spirits. There were many people who studied the field, but they didn't know how to heal and resolve a situation, at least not like mine. Out of desperation, I talked a medium named Bonnie into helping me. She was reluctant, and looking back, I realize she was scared. My case was beyond her skill and understanding, but her work with me was helpful.

I spent the night at her house and she performed an energy clearing on my aura, but could not protect me from the entity that was haunting me. She attempted to clear him, but she could only temporally banish his energy. He kept coming back, which frightened her.

That night, she left me to sleep on the couch while she slept in her bedroom with the door firmly shut and locked. I did everything I could to stay awake. I read and reread all her magazines, looked through her books, paced the floor, and pleaded with God to protect me and take away the entity problems. I was aware, and so was Bonnie, that I had to accept what was going on and face the being alone, and I had to do it with no one's help.

Around 3:00 a.m., I couldn't fight my exhaustion any longer since I hadn't gotten a decent night's sleep in several weeks. I finally drifted to sleep. The entity had been waiting. As soon as my consciousness and astral body entered that astral plane in my sleep, but before I entered a dream, the entity viciously attacked. I still remember how the blow to my chest felt even after all these years: the energy was cold, hard, black, and consuming.

He threw me down, sat on top of me and repeatedly began hitting me in the heart chakra or chest. I panicked. I pleaded with him to stop. I pleaded with God to stop him. I pleaded with my angels to intervene. Nothing happened. Nobody came. Then, after what seemed like an eternity, I heard a voice repeating a mantra in my mind: "I release into love, love sets me free, and I am one with God." I chanted this mantra repeatedly and in doing so, I relaxed. Instead of trying to protect myself by closing off, I opened. I opened my heart, my energy, and my mind.

The entity stopped hitting me in the heart chakra, and in-fact, he jumped off of me like I was hurting him. He left without another word or action. I knew I hadn't crossed him over to the Soul planes, but I accomplished something even more important: I conquered my fear enough to face my journey. Never again would I ignore what was happening and try to run away from it.

Shortly after the entity left, Bonnie woke up and came out of her bedroom. She performed another clearing on my aura and told me about my angelic council. Apparently, I had angel guides that were going to help me develop my skills and so on; they were just waiting for me to be ready. She said that they enjoyed working with me because I am so "willful" whatever that means. Anyway, they were waging bets on whether I would face my fear, which was a necessary step to even begin my training. All of my experiences up to this moment were to encourage me to face my fear rather than continue to struggle. The angels were waiting for me to have the courage to do the work. They had a sense of humor about the situation that I didn't really appreciate. Looking back, I see they protected me the whole time.

Well, long story short, that night was the beginning of four years of intense training with my council. Most of the time, it was unpleasant. When your teachers are in the spirit plane, training is often *spontaneous,* a nice way of saying inconvenient and *experiential*, a nice way of saying a confusing trial-and-error process.

That night was the last time I saw Bonnie. She couldn't help me any further, but she played an important role in my journey. She has long since passed into the spirit plane herself, and I wish her love and happiness.

Chapter Five

Four Years of Learning

In the beginning, I had a really poor attitude. I hated this part of my work and gifts. Your gifts come to you, not the other way around. One could argue that it's an amazing opportunity to be chosen to collaborate with the spiritual plane and it makes life more exciting. It took me many years to learn how to effectively interact with entities, ghosts, thought-forms and different kinds of energy - and yes, my life is interesting.

To clarify that while my 'intense' training was about four years in duration, I continue to learn and grow in my skills. I learn something new or gain a greater understanding of a concept all the time. My training escalated with a woman; a spirit guide, to be exact.

She announced her arrival into my life by sitting on the couch one evening while I was watching TV. She just sat there without saying a word. I wasn't sure who or what she was, so I said nothing and ignored her presence. Please understand, when you are bothered at night by spirits and work with them all day during healing sessions with clients, the last thing you want to do is talk to another one while you are trying to watch your favorite TV show. So, she said nothing, and I said nothing. Then she left as fast as she had arrived.

She came back, and it wasn't a joyful reunion. I was having a nice, bland, day-to-day stuff kind of dream when she rudely and abruptly yanked my astral body and consciousness from the dream and dumped me into one of the lower levels of the astral plane. It was a shock to my system.

It was pitch black and right out of a horror movie. I couldn't see anything, but I could hear and feel them. Beings and not the good kind surrounded me. Their whispers overwhelmed me like a thousand voices whispering all at once. Some would call it demon-speak. I put my hands over my ears to reduce the pain; it actually hurt even though my physical body was safely tucked away in my bed.

Immediately, recognizing I was out of place, the beings or entities crowded me, and the weight of their energy was like walking underwater across the floor of the ocean. And their hands, well, I will just say they were everywhere. I panicked.

I was so disoriented and terrified; I screamed. I can't remember if I made a sound when I screamed. The nasty sounds they made were what I remember. I am not sure how long this went on. A few seconds could easily feel like several minutes.

Once I managed to gain coherent thought, I prayed, or you could call it begging for help. At first, nothing: no light, no lessoning of the negative soup of energy I was experiencing, and no savior. I felt my panic rise even more. I did not know how to rescue myself. It was the worst, strongest, negative energy I had experienced thus far. There were too many of them. I had never encountered so many negative entities at once, not to mention they had the advantage of home-turf.

The blackness of the entities surrounded me like a thousand buzzing bees. The energy actually felt like a kind of static. It hurt, yet it was hard to grab onto. Then I heard her in my mind. She was repeating, "Make your mind as hard as granite and, like the bear, go deep within and find your strength." Her voice was like a beam of hope, and I focused on it. I wasn't sure exactly how to do what she requested, but it was figure it out or stay with the entities, which was not an option I could live with.

I ignored, as much as I could, the entities around me and I meditated. I brought my awareness to my breath and to the light within my heart. My focus was on love, joy, and memories of goodness. As I did so, my mind and spirit calmed. I remembered who and what I was. I focused on my Divinity gifted to me, and to you, by the creative life-force energy or God.

My energy shifted from a fear or low vibration to a higher light vibration and I broke free. I made the light within me brighter and brighter, getting stronger with every second. The entities scattered, and I returned to my physical body.

The spirit guide was waiting for me in my bedroom. She said, "Congratulations, you passed the test and now you are ready to begin the next level of your training." I didn't sleep the rest of the night. I had some hot calming tea and contemplated what she meant.

We worked together for several months. She was a woman of few words. She communicated through action, but she taught me about focus, strength, courage, and control over my emotions, especially fear.

I miss her. I know she had other charges/people to work with. I haven't seen her for years, but it wouldn't surprise me if she checks in on me once in a while. She had a grandmother-like energy about her: strong, wise, and no nonsense. She never gave me her name. It wasn't necessary for the work. She wasn't one to waste time or coddle. Just the thought of her makes me smile, though despite my first training session with her.

The astral plane contains several levels or dimensions. The one I experienced was a negative, low vibration and self-created by the human consciousness. One could assume it was hell, but that assumption suggests that someone or something traps a spirit. It's my understanding, from years of experience, that a spirit or being can free themselves from any negative energy or realm, just like I did if they feel worthy of and connect to the light within themselves. They are alive and, therefore; they are life-force energy created by the Divine.

My training continued. First, I dealt with manageable, low-level entities. The more negative encounter I experienced, the easier the work became. My mind adapted and my fear response diminished. I joked around to myself, "Hello darkness my old friend." Ha! But, in all seriousness, some attacks were brutal, and it's just one of those skills mastered by practicing. A practitioner gets better by doing and learning from his or her experience. That is why the spirit guide just dumped me into the pit with the entities. It was the fastest way for me to learn: sink or swim, baby.

I had several questions about the astral plane, entities, and why it was necessary for me and others to do the work. Those four years were educational. I needed to develop my skill or suffer the consequences of procrastination. I stopped resisting one of my life's purposes. If you are called to this type of work, you are more than capable.

Chapter Six

The Human Condition

Why are practitioners needed for clearing entities, ghosts, and so on? Why can't the angels do it? Well, to quote an angel when I asked these very questions, he said, "It's our job to keep the balance; it's not our job to clean up humanity's self-created negativity." Basically, it's our mess, so it's our responsibility.

Now, that is not to say the practitioner is abandoned to do the work on his or her own. The angels are very active and supportive in the healing and clearing process of negativity, and in fact, absolutely necessary. A practitioner actually needs the assistance of the Divine to accomplish the task. A partnership between humans and angels/guides achieves healing, transforming, and the clearing of negativity. Both contribute much needed, but unique skills and energy. One cannot do it without the other.

The reality that entities are self-created by humanity and consequently, our mess to clean up is not the only reason angels cannot rescue us from ourselves. The shadow-side of the ego generates entities. The shadow-side of the ego contains the individual's fear, anger, shame, and, in some cases, hatred. Angels or guides have such a lovely, exalted vibration that their energy is too high in frequency to connect with the low energy of entities without a bridge, and guess who provides the bridge: we do. Fortunately, every human has a shadow side, which makes us perfect for bridging the gap between the lower levels of the astral plane and the high levels of the soul planes. While it's true, we have a dark side, it's also true that we have a light side and the very fact that they coexist together allows us to effortlessly travel in all the realms: low and high.

Humans are flawed, but that is an intentional condition for experience and growth. Essentially, emotional and mental flaws are a common part of everyone's journey and are not concerning nor are they judged. Emotions are meant to be fluid–to come in–to process through and experience for learning–and then to flow out. Entities are by-products of the ego's inability to process these emotions and life's challenges in a healthy and functional way. If left to dysfunction for many decades, the emotions and mental mind-set can become extreme expressions of negative energy and an entity is created during the lifetime.

Life is a constant battle or interaction between the lower self and higher self every moment of every day. Do you respond with kindness or with a snarky verbal arrow because the person is getting on your nerves? Do you remember that the person you are interacting with is part of you in the big scope of life? It takes far more strength to love or show kindness than it does to hate, which is why many of us fail at it, especially when stressed or unhappy with our own lives. Note: mentally and emotionally failing while we are learning about self-awareness doesn't create an entity. Continuous and extreme negative behavior that causes damage to oneself and others over a long period is necessary. Keep in mind, this is a rarity.

Often I am asked, 'What can I do to prevent an entity or the negative energy given off by others from attaching to me?' I appreciate the question because many people walk around with attachments or even self-created thought-forms, (more about that later), and do not know that a negative spirit or that negative energy from others is amplifying their negative emotions and negative thoughts. They assume that it's just part of life and feeling emotion.

Processing difficult emotions is overwhelming, but it shouldn't become a lifestyle. A person is allowed bad days or terrible weeks during times of crisis, but contentment and healthy interactions with others are the norm rather than the exception.

To answer the above question about self-protection, I want to begin with the act of protecting oneself from negative entities or negative energy is an act of fear. Now, before you get all worked up, let me explain. When we encircle ourselves with white light for protection, instead of being the white light, through a lot of hard work and emotional integrity, we are saying to the outside source of energy that it has the power to hurt or influence us. Our actions send the message that we are weaker than the outside energy. Since we have access to an unlimited source of energy through the Divine, that belief is simply not true.

If a person can establish a strong connection with the light within or Divine within by choosing his or hers higher-self or the way of the light, in everyday situations living with integrity. That is a great start in preventing negative energy from attaching. I am aware, however; this is easier said than done.

It's part of the human condition to be burdened with fear of survival and to want everything of value to us as individuals. It takes a commitment to one's personal, spiritual journey and pursuing love, honor, and wisdom to fully buffer ourselves from outside negative energy. Turning personal fear into kindness is part of the transformation process, along with the understanding of personal boundaries, well-being, and sharing with others. Basically, protection from negative energy is many things, including self-mastery, relationship wisdom, and the overall evolution of the soul.

The higher in vibration one achieves or the more light one can contain and share, the stronger he or she becomes. Fear and insecurity must be present in someone's spirit or being in order for negative energy to connect with them.

But, since none of us have achieved self-mastership and therefore, mastery over life, there are many lessons and skills we can learn that greatly reduces our vulnerability to negative energy, so yeah, there's hope.

Chapter Seven

Awareness

Understanding our karma, our journey, and the resulting wisdom attained from the lessons creates a high vibrational being with less and less fear. Entities and negative energy need fear to attach to someone's aura. Without the fear, the person's spirit and aura are too high in vibration, which prevents negative energy attachment. No matter what our ego might want, we cannot fake the high vibration. It must be authentic. We need to do our best to be patient with divine timing, and take each moment with the information it presents to us, and make the right choice. This will bring us one step nearer to resolution or creation by allowing the wisdom of time to work issues out and unite all the components. There is no need for aggression, attachment, and pursuit. As we show up with a healthy mind-set and participate, we are doing our part in the situation.

We can transform the negative energy in the astral plane and in the Earth planes by transforming the fear within ourselves and by helping each other. It is the responsibility of humankind to address the energy that has been created out of fear. We misuse our power and hurt each other out of pain-stress-insecurity-ignorance, and fear. The massive amount of negative energy created by our toxic emotional and physical interactions affects all of us with one another. Entities, negative thought-forms, and blocks are all a result of humanity's issues.

Gratefully, we have help, lots of it. It is our birthright to be happy, express our creativity, and to claim our own living space, body, and energy. We do not need to stand by and be victimized by an entity or any other negative energy, even if we ourselves are still flawed and figuring things out.

There are several tools and resources to help us deal with the unexpected attachment or haunting. The first goal is to distinguish between what is our own negative energy and what is coming at us from someone else. Discernment, knowing ourselves, and knowing the energy of our environment is an essential skill. Assess the circumstances before taking action if a negative presence appears.

How the entity enters our life is important information. If we buy a new house or piece of land that is loaded with trauma, which amplifies negative energy and draws entities, the clearing process is less complicated than if we picked up the negative entity from someone else or during our own travels.

What are the signs of a negative energy being attached to us or present in our home?

Negative Entities cannot create an energy or emotion within us. They can, however, amplify and dramatize what is already there. As evolving souls having a human experience, we need to take responsibility for our own negativity and avoid the temptation of blaming others.

There are some common key elements that most hauntings or attachments include:

- A person will feel moodier with lower than normal energy.

- Relationship disagreements are more common, and they are amplified or taken out of context.
- A person's dreams might contain gross, violent, negative sexuality, or torture scenes and or experiences. Sometimes an entity takes a more direct approach and surrounds a person with heavy negativity that wakes him or her up, but just as often, they manipulate a person's dream to amplify the

negative emotions of hate, anger, fear, and shame. The dreams will contain content that, when awake, the dreamer questions, 'Where did that come from?" And of course, the traditional bad dream is always a winner for the entity. Do not forget, the more experienced ones are master manipulators. Nevertheless, a handful of bad dreams by themselves don't always mean an attachment.

- Our aura, our body, and the instincts given to us by the Divine know before our conscious mind, when something is in our space. We can call it animal instinct or intuitive instinct, but it's not based on a logical assessment, but rather a feeling or instinctual knowing. This awareness or information has its own language and communicates with the conscious mind through mental imagery, unease in the nervous system, anxiety, or a low grade of emotional discomfort. To put it simply, the body's nervous system is activated and a person will feel uneasy; this can manifest itself as an inability to sleep after being disturbed during the night, or a feeling of unease in a particular room or space during the day or night. It's important to be able to relax, day or night, in your own home, even if alone. If that is impossible, something is wrong and the situation or feelings need to be assessed.

- Another example is the feeling of depression, sadness, anger, fear, or just an overall feeling of heaviness in a space or after leaving that space or person.

- The sensation of someone standing right behind you, and the sensation of being watched.

- Extreme negative thought is another symptom. A person could have images of hurting themselves or another. Images of screaming matches or hurting someone else verbally are also manifestations of a negative influence if other symptoms are also present.
- A person will have difficulty creating positive life goals, feeling good, feeling happy, and an interestingly enough, an unwillingness to accept advice or help.

Not one of these signs alone is necessarily a sign of a negative entity, but if several occur together, it could be an indication of one being nearby. If, after careful consideration, it is determined an entity is attached to a person or a home, please do not discuss it. Entities listen and plan. Ask for help, but be brief about it and try to discuss the issue outside of the home.

Chapter Eight

Hope

If a person discovers he or she has an entity attachment or if he or she has a haunted house, there is hope. The best option is to find a healing practitioner that specializes in negative energy and house clearings. If, however, a person wants to clear the negative energy on his or her own, there are some helpful techniques. Nevertheless, allow me to recommend that getting help is the best course of action and if the task proves too difficult, don't be hesitant to seek professional assistance.

Everyone's relationship with the Divine and spirituality is unique and as long as those beliefs generate love and kindness, a person has a good chance at clearing negative energy. Still, a trained healing practitioner is the best person for the job. It's beneficial if a person understands the spirit planes, knows how to channel, amplify, and direct energy, as well as has an established relationship with the Divine through meditation and life experience. I'll continue this chapter by looking at it from the viewpoint of an experienced healing practitioner.

Like I mentioned, everyone has his or her unique, personal relationship with the Divine, so the guidance I give here is only one possibility and so modification from person to person is expected. To be successful, it is essential to have an unyielding, long-standing relationship with the Divine, angels, and spirit guides. Collaboration between a human and the Divine is necessary in order to clear an entity.

Even though a practitioner gets assistance from the Divine during a clearing, if that practitioner doesn't have his or hers life balanced and if there is chronic issues that disrupt alignment with the Divine within as well as without, the practitioner will fail at clearing the entity. He or she might succeed at temporarily banishing the being, but fail at crossing it over to the soul plane. The spirit will come back to haunt the one it was attached to and could also cause trouble for the practitioner.

I was just reminded of this problem this morning, right before I began writing for the day. A student of mine texted me and told me she thought she had an entity attachment. She went to a practitioner to have it cleared, but it came back to her. She believes the practitioner only succeeded in getting rid of it temporarily, so she came to me.

This is not uncommon. A practitioner still faces everyday experiences that challenge the Spirit/individual to either respond from the lower-self guided by the ego or the higher-self guided by the Divine within. Powerful emotions, such as anger, create the challenge. Self-mastery suggests that the individual has reached a level of emotional wisdom, not perfection, which creates a deep capacity to love and to be love's expression in a Divine, non-attached to outcome sort of way. Developing an inner-strength through a positive attitude in the face of life's challenges can bring about peace, integrity, emotional balance, and wisdom during difficult times. If we try our best to find the useful energy in the situation, we achieve a positive mindset.

If a practitioner hasn't reached some level of self-mastery over his or her emotions, he or she will banish entities more often than crossing them over. To keep an open and strong heart chakra, we must have genuine spiritual transformation and emotional integrity, regardless of what level of development we think we have reached. If the level of self-mastery isn't real, the practitioner's vibration is limited and, therefore, so is his or her ability. Still, having said that, some entities will take more time to cross over because their negative energy is well-established, experienced and strong or there is more than one. Often, I give myself a few days to a few weeks to clear all the negative energy just in case there are many.

Keeping in mind, self-mastery doesn't demand perfection; it simply requires love. A practitioner can be flawed and make mistakes with others, but if he or she has an open and willing heart to love, to learn, to be better, the high vibrations of love fill the practitioner's heart chakra and aura giving him or her the ability to create bridges between the realms, that allows lower vibrations to rise into the higher levels for healing. Pure intent and a willing, loving heart are all the power needed.

This cannot be manufactured or pursued like a goal. It blossoms within a practitioner over time, like a flower blooms in the sunlight. Developing the ability to traverse entities strengthens on its own timeline. The gift chooses the practitioner, not the other way around.

Chapter Nine

The Clearing Process

If a person wants to attempt the clearing on his or her own, this can be very empowering, and even if he or she decide to get help from a practitioner, taking part in the process is powerful and helps to ensure success, especially if the case, is a house haunting versus an individual attachment. It's my experience that if a house is haunted, there is usually an individual attachment as well. One individual within the household is usually chosen by the entity to be the primary focus. A person can have an individual entity attachment that they picked up from another person or another house and bring that home to his or her own house. With a haunted house, the entity is usually there before the people move in. In the case of a personal attachment, the person brings the entity into the home, but the entity usually stays pretty close to one individual.

House Hauntings

The house will need to be cleared on three levels or planes of existence: the physical, the energy level or energy blueprint of the house, and the astral level, which is where the entity resides.

Step One: Assessment

Entities have a tendency to gather in the areas of a house with the lowest energy, activity and light, like a basement, but this isn't always the case. They can hangout where there are frequent arguments, places of trauma, in bedrooms or even just corners of a house or hallways. It all depends on the energy balance of the house. It is important to use and nurture all areas of a home to keep the energy positive and resistant to negative energy. The homeowner must claim the space in the entire home with his or her personal, positive energy.

Step one is to assess and measure the energy in the home. With a pendulum or simply use your instincts, walk through each room of the house, including the basement by yourself. Other people can be distracting during this process. If a practitioner is using a pendulum, he or she needs to measure each corner, center of the room, closets or alcoves, and any items that draw your attention. The pendulum will move in a small clockwise circle if the energy is positive. Any other rotation suggests imbalanced energy. Also, look for cold spots or areas that make you feel uncomfortable.

Step Two: Clean and Declutter

Our stuff holds energy. A clearing on the energy level of a house won't hold very long if the physical level of the house is dirty, neglected, and overly cluttered. A homeowner doesn't need to be perfectly clean or organized. Any house requires good maintenance and a positive flow of energy. The house should contain items that are both cherished and needed. Everything else is unwanted clutter. If any piece of furniture or item is associated with negative feelings, get rid of it. Basements and attics need to be cleaned as well. Neglecting these areas can give negative energy a place to gather overtime and disrupt the positive energy flow of the rest of the house.

Cleaning the house on the physical level allows the homeowner to claim the space and put his or her energy into the house. This is very important. We need to not only own our individuality in life, but claim the space we live in. If we don't, the energy from others and from the environment will do it for us. To have a home is a blessing, so respect your home, and it will nourish you in return.

Step Three: Gather the Tools

This is where individual spirituality and belief become part of the process. Since everyone is so different in this area, I will provide general suggestions of what tools to use offering a starting point.

Candles for house altar and tea candles for each room

Items that represent spiritual beliefs like a cross or an angel figurine

Herbs: sage, pine, sweet grass, myrrh, rosemary, rose petals, and cedarwood are just a few of the many herbs that are considered cleansing.

Sea salt for the altar, windows, doors, around the outside of the house and for each room

Items that represent the four elements, such as salt or crystals for earth, water for water, wind chimes, pipes, feathers for air and candles or knives for fire

Drum: to break up blocked and stagnant energy

Sage to smudge the rooms

Bells or singing bowls to raise vibrations

Blessed water to sprinkle around the space, anoint items, doors, etc.

Altar: A kitchen or dining room table is a good place to set up an altar. A tray works just as well, too. The altar is going to represent the intention of the homeowner. The altar will need items that represent the four elements, the Divine, candles, and the intent. Setting up an altar is like saying a prayer to the Divine, asking for guidance and blessings.

Step Four: House Clearing Ceremony

The homeowner, the practitioner, or both can do the house clearing ceremony after the physical cleaning of the house is completed. They can perform it before the astral clearing that clears out the actual entity, at the same time or after. In most cases, I clear out the entity or entities while the homeowner does the house clearing ceremony. If they are uncomfortable doing the ceremony, I clear the astral level/entity first and then I clear out the energy level of the house with the house clearing ceremony.

On a side note: If a practitioner is good at astral travel, he or she can remove the entity from a distance and does not need to be on location. I prefer to clear this way since it allows me to be on the same energetic level as the entity. They are easier to tract, surprise, and crossover. Again, I will remind you that engaging in a conversation with an entity is not useful and only serves to distract or delay the practitioner.

In the center of the house or just outside the front door, take a moment to say a prayer and call the Divine energy to assist in the clearing process. The prayer can be any style the practitioner or homeowner prefers as long as it invites the Divine: Goddess/God, angels, spirit guides etc., and the elements. Inviting the elements and or positive energies of the directions they govern is useful because elemental energy forms all life.

Example of House Clearing Prayer:

Dear Mother/Father God, Jesus Christ the Son, and the Holy Spirit as one. Dear Angels, Spirit guides, and Animal totems, the healing forces of Reiki, Karuna, and Urevia, the sun, the moon, the stars, and of the North and element of Earth, of the East and element of Air, of the South and element of Fire, and of the West and the element of water to please help us with this healing and clearing today as we give ourselves and this process over to the Divine to guide, bless, and empower. Thank you for hearing and considering our prayer. Amen.

It doesn't need to be fancy, but there are people gifted with beautiful words (I am not one of them), so look around and use what feels right.

After the prayer, a drum or bell is used to begin the ceremony. Move to the house alter and speak the intention of the house clearing out loud and light the center candle. Make sure that the intention and altar are already established by this point.

Starting in the North or East, use a drum or bell to walk around the room or space, moving clockwise, beat the drum or ring the bell intending to break up negative energy. I would rather use a drum than a bell, but whatever the practitioner feels is most effective will work as long as all areas of the house are included.

It is common to hear the drum change tones as it encounters negative energy. When this change takes place, spend more time in that area of the house.

After the drumming is complete, it's time to clear away the negative energy that has been broken up and disbursed by the drum. This is where practitioners are more effective than the homeowner because someone attuned a certified practitioner to healing energies like Urevia, Usui Reiki, Karuna, and so on. Just like a healing, each room needs to be cleared and charged with the intention that all negative energy go to the light for transformation. If a homeowner is facilitating the house clearing, he or she can access the love and light each person carries in the heart chakra and beam that into the room, filling it with high vibrations and carrying the negative energy to light. Regardless of the method, each room needs to be cleared and charged with positive energy.

Clear and charge one room at a time and then place sea salt in each corner of the room to hold and protect the positive energy. In the center of the room, light a tea candle and say a prayer for that room specifically. For example, if it's a bedroom, the prayer might request that the room be protected and filled with peaceful energy.

Blessing of the room is next. Take spring water that was blessed through prayer and sprinkle a little in the four directions and center of the room, asking that the Divine bless and empower the room, filling it with love and light. Room by room; continue the process by repeating each step.

Drum: break up the energy

Clearing and charging: removing negative energy and filling the room with positive

Sea Salt: place a little in each corner to hold and protect the positive energy in the room

Tea Candle: light the candle with an intention prayer and as the candle burns, it sends energy towards that intention or request for the room

Bless the Room: using blessed, spring water sprinkle a little in the four directions and in the center of each room while asking the Divine to bless the room.

Step Five: Closing the Ceremony

Take a moment to go over every room in the house with the pendulum. The rotation should be clockwise in all areas of the house. If not, go back to the area of concern and use the drum and clear the area again. Take your time! It is important that the person clearing the house is calm and content. The practitioner or homeowner needs to enjoy the ceremony and be grateful for the opportunity. The more positive a person feels, the more effective he or she is at clearing negative energy, so be happy, be content, and be at peace.

Find the most center location of the house and say a blessing and protection prayer for the house and surrounding land. Next, when heading to the entrance, lay a line of sea salt across the doorframe or threshold to keep any negative energy generated by others from entering the house. With either a drum or bell, play three notes while saying a closing prayer and blessing. The closing prayer should show gratitude and appreciation towards the Divine, thanking all the energies that assisted and empowered the house clearing ceremony.

If a practitioner wants to add a little extra protection to the property, he or she can complete the closing process by using sea salt on every windowsill, circling every sink drain, and circling the entire foundation of the house on the outside. This is only necessary for extreme hauntings or extreme negative energy.

This is a basic outline of a house clearing ceremony. Using one's intuition, spiritual beliefs, and personal style is helpful, so I encourage everyone to expand on this ceremony.

Step Six: Entity Clearing

Whether the house is being haunted by an entity or ghost, this part of the process can be completed prior to, during, or after the house clearing ceremony. The most ideal situation would be to have the entity cleared before the house clearing, if possible, within 24 hours. Each situation is unique, and trusting one's instincts is the best approach.

As I stated earlier, I usually clear entities from a distance using an astral travel and healing technique. I find it easier because I do not have to worry about my physical body, nor do I need to be physically at the location of the haunting, which is helpful to the clients that live far away from me. However, if a person lacks astral travel experienced, he or she shouldn't attempt astral travel entity clearing.

What Do You Need to Know?

No drama please

Many people make the situation worse by trying to talk to the entity or spirit. They want to know its story or they want to nurture it. Please resist the need to figure it out or understand why it is earth bound; for two reasons: They lie, and it does not matter why the entity is there. In a nut-shell, a person shouldn't engage in a conversation with an entity. It doesn't change the outcome and is a waste of time. After the Divine beings of light reunite the entity with the light, it works through its healing issues.

Fear–what fear?

It is impossible to eradicate fear. Instead, try to remember the truth: fear is an illusion. We are not alone, and love creates life-force energy. Everything that exists is part of that life-force energy. Also, ignoring the presence of an entity will often prolong your suffering. Just deal with it.

Did you see that?

This might sound confusing, but the spirit world is not an exact science, therefore, what the mind perceives isn't always accurate. Think, Symbolic Intuition. Some of what a person sees, not all, is the mind projecting a symbolic image that represents the entity's vibration. The mind projects an image of the entity that best describes the mind's interpretation of the entity's energy. It's the mind's way of trying to understand what it's processing or perceiving. Basically, not everything a person sees is literal. Fear can lead to someone over-exaggerating what they're experiencing. Seeing the entity is not as important as following your body's instincts. Clarity improves with experience, so just keep practicing.

Trust your instincts

A person's body and dreams often sense something is wrong before the conscious mind becomes aware of the disturbance. During the day, a person will feel something watching him or her or feel uncomfortable in certain areas of the house. At night, dreams will be unusually stressful or ugly. A person might find him or herself in gross or torturous situations while dreaming. Instincts and the subconscious mind are trying to talk to the conscious mind should either of these issues arise. The most common cause of these experiences is an entity attachment.

Entity Clearing

- **Meditate–please for the love of God–meditate.** Any meditation will do as long as some form of meditative practice develops a close relationship with the Divine. Meditation also strengthens and focuses intention/will when clearing entities and supports healthy well-being.

- **Mantras.** Making use of two kinds of mantras is beneficial: one to elevate a person's vibration and empower the connection to the Divine, and another to clear entities.

- **Angels and Healing Energy.** Keeping in touch with the angels can be of great help. The stronger a person's relationship is with them, the more they can assist with the entity clearing process. Next, a practitioner should give him or herself daily healings, which will empower and clear the chakras and always, before clearing an entity.

- **Learn how to astral project and travel.** Make sure to always clear entities by using the astral body in the astral plane. The physical body is too heavy in vibration and just gets in the way. This is another reason meditation is very important. To master projecting onto the astral plane and sustain focus for long durations, a practitioner or person must practice. Visualizing and spending time with the angels during meditation is a good way to practice this technique, so is giving astral travel healings.

- **Clearing a haunted house from a distance is best, leaving the body behind.** Go into a meditative state and clear the entity from a distance before the house clearing appointment. The same rule applies when an entity attaches to a person; if a practitioner can clear the entity from a distance before or after a healing, it is more effective. It is possible to clear onsite or in the moment by entering a meditative state and projecting onto the astral plane, leaving the body behind, clearing the entity. However, I discourage on-site clearings because there are too many distractions. However, some practitioners prefer on-site clearing and find it an effective method.

- **A person should avoid attempting to clear entities in the dream state even if he or she wakes up inside the dream, turning it into a lucid dream.** Wake up! As soon as a practitioner realizes the dream is unusual, he or she should wake up. Once awake, a practitioner needs to take his or her time. Go into a meditative state, call to the angels, ask for help, say the mantras and run the healing energy through the aura. After the practitioner is ready, return to the dream with astral projection, attempt to identify the entity manipulating the dream, and then clear it.

- **No such thing as linear time.** A practitioner can astral project back in time to clear an entity if, and only if, he or she knows when and where to go. For example, a practitioner can go back into a dream after he or she has awoken and clear the entity. The timing does not need to be exact, but the location does. Also, entities can come and go. A practitioner needs to have patience. Clearing entities is a process, so keep trying until desired results are achieved.

- **Drop offs. A person with an entity attachment can bring it into another person's house.** It's rare because an entity usually stays with its host. It takes a few days before someone realizes an entity is hanging around in his or her house or, in the case of a healing session, has located the practitioner after he or she has given its host a healing.

- **Two-week rule.** When clearing one or more entities, waiting a few weeks for the energy to resettle before clearing again offers clarity and perspective.

Clearing Basics for Low Level Entities

Go into a meditative state

1. Call to the angels for help

2. Channel healing energy to self

3. Repeat favorite mantras

4. Focus, the mind

5. Go into sacred center or heart chakra–always start from here on the astral plane and always return to this center when finished

6. With angels, animal totems, and spirit guides by the practitioner's side, he or she calls to the Divine life-force energy within expanding the size of the aura.

7. With help from the Divine guides, locate the entity

8. Once found, a practitioner chants the clearing mantra and extends a bright white light from his or her heart

chakra to the angel's heart chakra, and then to the entity's heart. When the beam of Divine light enters the entity's heart center, it pulls from within the entity the Divine life-force energy from which it's created from. Drawing on Divine light energy from within, the entity raises its vibration, allowing it to ascend to the soul planes. Basically, the truth sets it free: the entity is part of the light as well.

9. Engage the Merkaba, (the three dimensional six-pointed star and one of the sacred geometric shapes that is part of everyone's aura and in all other lifeforms). As it spins -it floods the entire space with white light.

10. With the power and will of all, take the entity to the transitional plane, which often looks like a beautiful field of flowers or another nature-like scene and leads to the various soul planes where it's met by loved ones, its Divine self, and or angels.

11. Return to your sacred center or heart chakra–thank your guides and relax

Wait, a few days to a few weeks to see if the entity has successfully cleared. Of course, clear sooner if you are attacked again, but if not, wait a few weeks. Sometimes entities travel in packs and you may need to clear more than one over several weeks. Tarot cards and pendulums are helpful tools to use if you want more information and confirmation of a successful clearing.

Mantras

Entity Clearing Mantra:

I am love

I am light

I am compassion in action

United with Goddess/God I stand

Calling thee home to the promise land

You are worthy

You are loved

And you are one of us

By the will of the Divine

Pain is erased

Chains are broken

Leaving no trace

From my heart to your heart

Goddess/God calls forth the Divine within

And we are one

St. Germain's Mantra: I am Light

I am light, glowing light,

Radiating light, intensified light,

God consumes my darkness,

Transmuting it into light

This day I am a focus of the central sun,

Flowing through me is a crystal river,

A living fountain of light

That can never be qualified by human thought or feeling

I am an outpost of the Divine

Such darkness that has used me is swallowed up by the mighty river of light. I am

I am, I am, I am light

I live, I live, I live in light

I am lights fullest dimension,

I am lights purest intention

I am light, light, light

Flooding my being and the world with light and love

Repeat this mantra at least three times and up to twelve times in one setting. It clears and centers the mind, emotions, and energy field.

Entity Clearing Level II

Ego Evolution

- **House Clearing and more Advanced Negative Entities**

- **Astral Projection**

The Ego:

1. Emotions are fluid–to come in- to process through us, so that we can enjoy and/or learn from life and each other.

2. Holding grudges by making excuses to hold position or nurse pain by reliving emotional and mental perspective over and over is a negative expression of the ego, and will only create low vibrations in the heart. This pattern can be emotionally addictive. Whether our pain is justified isn't up for debate. Of course it is. We need to use our life experiences and give them a productive purpose.

3. How hard is for you to say you are sorry, especially if you believe you are right?

4. A practitioner must learn how to truly let go, accept, forgive, and to go further by promoting goodwill and keeping one's heart open.

5. Staying angry or holding grudges over hurt feelings invites entities into a person's space.

6. The more evolved and healthier the ego, the more powerful the healer. If a practitioner is having trouble clearing an entity, he or she needs to keep trying; however, to clear even the most negative entity on the first try, a practitioner needs to continuing work on integrating his or her ego with the Divine-self.

House Clearing and Really Negative Entities

1. Always give the client a healing first. (I only charge for the healings. The entity work is free because some entities require more time and I never want money to be an issue).

2. Like previously written, the house needs to be cleared on three levels: the client needs to declutter and give away old, low energy stuff along with giving the house a superb cleaning. Redecorating or moving furniture

may also be helpful. Second level: give the client simple instructions on how to bless his or her home. A basic cleansing starts with a blessing prayer–drum every room–sage every room–light a tea candle in every room–a sprinkle of sea salt in every corner of every room–gratitude & blessing prayer. This process empowers the client to claim his or her space/home and nourishes it with positive energy. *Refer to the house clearing section in previous chapters for a full description of the process.

3. The third level clearing is the most important and needs to be spontaneously performed. Some of the best tools a practitioner has are the element of surprise and the ability to go back in time. Performing the house clearing after the client's healing is the most effective. A practitioner shouldn't tell the client when he or she will perform the clearing on the house. If they know, odds are the entity will know too. Later, in the middle of the night, the practitioner's angels will wake him or her up to perform the house clearing at the right moment.

Astral Projection:

1. Once the angels have awoken the practitioner, he or she can remain in bed or get up and sit in his or her favorite meditative space and position.

2. Repeat the "I am Light mantra" three to twelve times. TAKE YOUR TIME.

3. A practitioner connects with and utilizes the healing energies they are attuned to. Draw the healing symbols in each direction and the middle of the room to fill the space with light.

4. Meditate and enter the heart chakra. Always begin and end trips on the astral plane in the heart chakra. This chakra governs the astral body and is the most effective and safest way to travel on the astral plane. Stepping out of the body or using the cord technique is unnecessary.

5. Once in the heart chakra, the practitioner prays and calls to the angels, guides, animal totems, and his or hers spiritual Divine beings.

6. Once everyone has assembled, a discussion detailing a plan is organized. When all are ready, a staircase will appear with a white door at the top. This door takes the practitioner to the house of the client on the astral plane.

7. At first, the practitioner should be outside of the house to take an assessment, looking at it from several feet away.

8. Enter the most negative space first, and if possible, focus on the most negative entity first.

9. Refer to the clearing mantra in previous pages. The practitioner intentionally merges his or her heart chakra and energy with angels and the greater Divine/God. As one large light, all connect to the entity's heart chakra. Together, all cross over the being to the soul's transitionary plane, as previously detailed. The practitioner and the Divine beings of light release the heart chakra energy, allowing the entity to reunite with loved ones and so on.

10. Practitioner and Divine beings/angels return to clear the client's house as needed.

11. When finished, the practitioner returns to the white door that leads to his or her heart chakra.

12. In the heart chakra, the practitioner takes a few minutes to cleanse energy and discuss the events with the angels or beings of light.

13. It may take a few rounds of clearings for everything to be removed. Allow a few weeks for this process and use the tarot cards to confirm. If there are more entities to clear, they will make their presence known either by attacking the client or, more likely, by attacking the practitioner.

The evolution of the practitioner's ego determines the quality of vibration in the heart chakra and how effective he or she will be at clearing extreme negative entities. If a practitioner needs to clear the same location or same entity several times, he or she should ask for reinforcements to come and help.

Chapter Ten

Experience

Experience is the best teacher. With experience, a practitioner gains wisdom, strength, and effectiveness. The laws of the physical world don't apply to the spiritual realms, which can be perplexing, so go with the results. The entity will either be gone or not, and if not, the practitioner tries again. If that doesn't work, the practitioner can and should seek help. Joining forces with other professionals is a prudent and powerful choice when necessary.

I take a pause here and stress entity work should not be for ego gratification. Do not seek it out and if it should cross your path once or twice, that is still not enough of a reason to pursue it. Entity clearings are a calling for individuals that have the skill-set for such healing work. It is not for every practitioner, and it's not that much fun either. The work can be inconvenient, exhausting, scary, and highly specialized. That said, every person on the planet is capable of such healing work and has a right to choose what energy enters his or her space and life. The frequency of entity encounters will indicate to a practitioner if the work is for him or her. Coming across this kind of work a few times is normal, but consistent interaction over several months or years is a sign for a practitioner to pursue mastery in this area of the healing arts.

In the chapters ahead, I'll be relating some of my own encounters to put forward a range of examples of entity clearing/healing work. My experiences will differ from other practitioners because we all bring our own belief systems, history, and perspectives to each encounter. The results obtained are what matters most. We are either helping each other heal and grow, contributing to this world with positive goodwill or we are not.

I have been clearing entities now for almost thirty years as of this writing. I'm flabbergasted by how much remains to be discovered. Many of the experiences are beyond my complete understanding. The spiritual world is far too great and complex for my teeny, tiny intellect. I let the time-tested results be my guide. Even so, I am sure the depth of my understanding in all situations is lacking despite my successes. I have learned to trust the process even with insufficient information, and I take the path of light and love to the best of my ability.

I share my experiences to offer some insight, such as it is, into the spiritual world. Keep in mind, as you read, these spiritual events are from my perspective and, therefore, from my interpretation. Another practitioner or person may experience the same event differently; not at all unlike two different perspectives about one conversation.

Remember, our mind creates an intellectual bridge with the spiritual world through telepathic thought, imagery, and the individual's belief system, and previous experiences. In short, the intent of the energy is the same, but the spiritual language used to communicate the intent will vary from person to person.

The experiences have all become a blur with the passing of the years. The work has become so normal for me, that I have forgotten many clearing unless something jogs my memory. I will say that even though it has become normal, I still find it my least favorite and yet most satisfying part of my work. My least favorite because the entities always reveal themselves at the most inconvenient times for me and satisfying, because I know the work is important.

When I first accepted entity clearing as part of my healing work, I made a big production out of it. In doing so, initially, I made it more work. Yet, I think it was a necessary part of my journey.

I was still lacking confidence and experience, so I needed a little extra ritual and support. Before every clearing, I would spend a long time meditating and performing mini protection ceremonies. Looking back, I needed this at the time. I was working on elevating my confidence and vibration to a greater level, so it was beneficial in giving me a little boost.

I will begin with a clearing called the Black Hawk. This clearing stands out because of the negative energy generated by an entity actually manifested in the physical plane, which is unusual. Only a tiny percentage of entity clearings manifest in physical form. Most of them are just felt by the individual or they are mild manifestations such as lights coming on and off, door slamming or strange, powerful smells are some examples. The Black Hawk clearing went beyond mild irritations.

Chapter Eleven

The Black Hawk

I was meditating in the morning, going through my normal process and, within the meditation, a new animal totem appeared. It was a bear named Omar. Looking back, this was my first warning, especially given that he said the angels sent him to protect me and my home. I am always grateful for extra support, so I didn't think too much of it. As a reminder here, animal totems are spirit guides that take on the image and energy of an animal to convey a message and to represent their energy and purpose. Also, it's common for the angels to use animals both in spirit and in the physical to communicate with you.

It started with Christine. She is a client that booked a healing session with me because she was going through a difficult divorce and was also experiencing some haunting energy in her house. The negative energy bothered Christine at night and she also felt uncomfortable or tense during the day. She was experiencing strong negative emotions, but she thought the divorce created most of those feelings. I approached her session like I do with every session: I started with a healing and wellness techniques to calm her mind and emotions.

When I give a healing, it transmutes negative energy, clears away accumulated emotional and mental stress, opens the chakra systems, balances the nervous system and rejuvenates the body and spirit of a person. However, there is one side effect: If the person has an attachment of any kind, the healing sessions raises the vibration of the person's energy field or aura, balances emotions, and clears the mind, which inevitably dislodges the attachment, breaking the connection.

As you might imagine, an entity dislikes being disconnected from its host. They usually retaliate by going after the healer. The attack often takes place within one to three days after the healing session with the client. In Christine's case, it was a little different. She lives in a different state than I, so we did our sessions over the phone combined with astral travel healing work.

Christine called me at her appointed time and we were discussing what was going on in her life when I saw it right outside my office window: a black hawk. Now, I love birds! I have several as animal totems including the Red Tail Hawk. I love birds so much that my yard feels empty without them, so I feed them bird seed all year, just so I can see and hear them in my environment. Well, I was gazing outside the window while Christine was going over the negative details of her divorce and a black hawk perched on a branch just a few feet from the window.

At first, I was so excited. Imagine a large black hawk just a few feet from where I was sitting. It was like a dream come true for me, but then, after a few minutes, I felt it. This hawk just stared at me eye to eye without moving. Its energy felt off to me. Something wasn't right. I couldn't put my finger on it. Then Christine said something drawing my attention to her and what she was saying. I wanted to make a note of it, so I looked away from the window to write it down. When I looked back up, the hawk had vanished. I continued the healing session with Christine without further incidence. I forgot about the hawk and went about my life. After all, up to this point, I had never seen an entity have the power and now-how to manifest an animal form in the physical world. I might have read about the possibility somewhere, but unless I experience it firsthand, I withhold judgment.

A few days later, I was heading into town to buy some groceries, and there it was again: the black hawk. He was perched on a tree branch that grew close and over the road where it curved. He was just looking at me as I slowed down to take the curve. I thought, 'it can't be." I was about 12 miles from my house, but there he was again, staring at me with those black eyes. He watched me pass until I was out of sight. Okay, I thought. That was creepy.

While I was driving, I decided. I was going to do some research when I arrived home. The state of Michigan has a variety of hawks that inhabit the region. However, a jet black hawk is not one of them.

In the meantime, while I was trying to figure out the black hawk, I was gradually clearing out negative entities from Christine's home at night. The cause of the multiple entities present was due to the abundance of negative emotions and actions, which created a negative atmosphere that was attractive. It can take several days to clear a home and the people living in the space, if there is more than one entity, because they like to hide and come back later if they see a practitioner clearing away one of their peers.

Focusing again on the black hawk, when I arrived home after grocery shopping, I told my husband about the very unusual black hawk sighting on the side of the road, and that it looked like the same black hawk I had previously seen outside my office window. This was the first time I mentioned either sightings to my husband. He responded by saying he saw it, too. Apparently, he was coming home a few days ago and as he was pulling up to the garage, there was a black hawk perched on the roof of the garage just staring at him. He said they stared at each other for a few moments and then it flew off. I thought, 'okay, now I know something is not right about this hawk and it wasn't my imagination.'

I took a proactive approach. While I was evaluating the situation, I became aware that the black hawk was linked to the negative energy I was eradicating from Christine's home. It felt like it was studying me, looking for a weakness. And indeed, it was. I didn't want to wait for the energy manifesting the black hawk to attack me on its terms, so I went after it.

The element of surprise would be my greatest asset, and I chose the timing of my strike very carefully. I went back in time. I had the opportunity to do so because I knew the exact time and place where the black hawk would be present. Knowing the time and date of Christine's appointment before going back in time was crucial, and thankfully, I had that information.

I guided myself into a deep meditation and, with my astral body, traveled into the astral plane. I brought to my mind the exact place and moment I saw the black hawk. Directing my spirit to that location, I watched, without being seen, the situation. Observing the hawk from this advantage point, the astral plane, I discovered an important fact about the hawk: It simply was a projection of the entity it was attached. It wasn't the entity's entire energy, and most likely, the entity had to go into a deep meditation himself to accomplish the projection. He was using the hawk representation in a way similar to how I was using my astral body to transit and inhabit the astral plane.

This was the first time I had seen such a skill in action from an entity. Most of the time, they are identified by their negative energy and lack of drive to practice and perfect such skills, yet I was mistaken in my initial thought. Some can be far more cunning and manipulative than expected.

I spent some time observing the hawk from my hidden vantage point, and after I gathered all the information I could; I projected white light from my heart chakra to the black hawk. The light took it by surprise and it was instantly pissed-off, but it left. I traveled back to my physical body and went about my day.

I knew that my banishment of the black hawk could bring about some consequences, and it did. While entities are active during the day, influencing the space and people's thoughts and energy, they do most of their work in a person's dream state. There is one very important reason for this: they can access your astral body.

While we are awake, our consciousness is in the physical plane and, mostly, distracted by everyday life and obligations. However, while we sleep, there is no such distraction and our astral body leaves our physical body processing information, emotions, and experiences gathered by our mind during the day. The subconscious stores most of the information when we are awake, and we process the information in the dream state through the astral body. So, every night we enter the astral plane, the same plane that hosts entities and other spirits.

Most people are safe in their dream state. If someone has an entity attachment, this can cause issues because it gives the entity the ability to enter the dream state and alter it, thus affecting the dreamer's experience.

Many years ago, I learned how to wake myself up 'within' and 'from' a dream-state. I can wake myself up on demand, staying within the dream-state, also known as lucid dreaming, or I can wake myself up all the way and return to my physical body. I practiced this skill for years until it became as easy as breathing. It has saved my ass on multiple occasions, and my run in with the black hawk entity was no exception.

I was dreaming a regular, boring, everyday dream, and then it changed. In the dream, I found myself walking down a county road at night. As I was walking down the road in the dark, my instincts let me know something wasn't right. The road was empty except for a few old abandon cars on the side of the road. It felt weird. As soon as my instincts sent the alarm, I woke up my conscious mind within the dream state. Note: in a regular dream-state, the subconscious mind generates the dream experience.

I became consciously aware I was dreaming, meaning I was awake within the dream. Learning this technique was an important part of my training. I wasn't exactly sure of what was going on at first, so I stopped walking, pausing by one of the old, abandoned cars. To my left, I heard the screech of a hawk. As I heard a noise, I looked up to see the black hawk soaring close to the road and close to me, making its presence known. It continued to fly into the darkness, out of sight.

My gaze was on the hawk, so I didn't see the two entities behind me until it was too late. They both grabbed me and dragged me into one of the abandon cars. I am assuming they used the car to trap me since it was more confining space than the open road. They both proceeded to assault me with an aggressive frenzy. The goal was not only to gross me out, but to keep me from focusing my mind and will-power, which would have allowed me to free myself within the dream-state. It worked. I couldn't free myself from the dream for several minutes. Finally, I heard myself say, "Fuck!" and I experienced a wave of emotion that gave me the strength to will my astral body/spirit to return to my physical body and wake up in my bedroom.

I sat up and went over the astral experience, going over every detail. As I did so, I discovered a third entity; the one that sent the black hawk. The two that attacked me were the underlings, and the third entity was the leader. So, there were three. By attacking me, they gave me the exact location and time of where they would be.

I gathered to me my guides, angels, the Divine within and without, and the healing energies.

Together, we traveled back in time, back to the dream, and began the clearing process. There are several approaches a practitioner can take. Early in this writing, I gave a general outline of the clearing process. The method I use has developed over the years and works for me, but each practitioner must find his or her own path.

Going back in time is easy if a practitioner knows the where and when. Linear time is a measurement of the passing of time in the physical world. The angels, guides and I merged our energy together and then, with love and focused intent, we went back in time, using my connection to the entities formed by the dream experience.

The connection brought us to the very edge of the dream, which allowed us to observe without being noticed. We could locate all three entities involved. We turned to each other and merged our energies, creating a beam and channel of brilliant, love-life-force energy of the Divine, and as one, we beamed this energy into the heart chakras of each entity. There is no discussion. There doesn't need to be. The Divine energy clearly communicates that every being is part of the life-force energy that creates all life. Therefore, we truly are one. With this universal truth, we merge our combined energies with the entities and transported them to the soul plane where they reunite with their higher-self and loved ones. Now, some entities have little consciousness and as soon as they enter the soul plane, the energy immediately dissipates. This is especially true with negative thought-forms.

It is very difficult to put into words a process that is so profound, spiritual, loving, and magical. The practitioner or person involved in this miraculous process needs to be happy, healthy, and able to channel high vibrational energy since it's the human practitioner that is used as the connecter and bridge between the realms. Again, a reminder, everyone is capable of this skill.

These three were the last entities associated with the Christine case. It's customary for me to stay diligent for a few weeks after a clearing to ensure I have crossed all entities over. I do not consider a case complete until a few weeks go by without further incidence of any kind. Gratefully, Christine's case resolved, and I was happy to see it finished and gone.

Chapter Twelve

The Unicorn

Okay, this might sound a little out-there, I know it does, but it happened and therefore, it's a possibility that it could or has happened to someone else. The stories I'm sharing are not arranged in chronological order. Some of these experiences happened in decades ago, and some are more recent. As a practitioner's skill develops, he or she might encounter comparable encounters as he or she delves into the vast range of astral experiences accessible.

I have a unicorn for one of my animal totems. Yes, I know how that sounds, but one of my guides takes the form of a unicorn when she works with me. She has never changed her form. Remember, an animal totem is a spiritual energy that takes on the form of an animal to express its purpose and vibration.

Several years into my healing and teaching practice, I saw a unicorn during one of my morning meditations. She just showed up. She would come and visit me on and off over the years, but always during meditation and prayer and never in any other way. We developed a friendship, and she guided and supported me through many emotional experiences. I felt very fortunate to be blessed with the presence of this spirit guide.

Gradually, she worked with me, along with two other animal totems and the angels during entity clearings. She offered her pure love energy to empower the process, and help me connect to the love I carry, and so do you, within me. She is exceptional, and I love her dearly.

One night I was dreaming and found myself awaken, but still on the astral plane of my house. The dream had stopped, and I was lucid dreaming. I had just finished teaching a healing class the previous day with a group of students. One of them dropped off some entity baggage, which can happen during the attunement process. When a student goes through the attunement, it's equivalent to a very deep and strong healing session. It raises the student's vibration and clears out old negative energy. The student's healing process resulted in a few entities being left behind.

I found myself fully awake, in the astral plane, and completely out of my body. I looked around the room and saw a few shadowy figures moving quickly around me. They encircled me. Now, at this point, I should've gone back into my body and gather my spirit guides, etc. and then return to clear the entities later when I had help with me. Well, I got cocky. I didn't wake myself up. Instead, I took out my sword (this is a symbolic manifestation of the light or Divine within me that I sometimes use), and attempted to take care of them myself.

I was getting my ass kicked! I was too distracted. There were too many of them. I fell backward, landing on the floor with my sword in my hand next to me. Then the most wonderful thing happened, and it hasn't happened since; my chest started feeling really warm and the center of my heart chakra suddenly expanded. It felt not only hot, but I could actually see a swirl of energy appear on my chest.

This is the magical part: a small unicorn flew out of my heart chakra into the room and expanded to its full size. I didn't even know something like this was possible, not even on the astral plane. At first I was shocked, stunned even. I sat there a moment, trying to wrap my brain around what had just happened. I mean, it was amazing! Really unbelievable! I was instructed telepathically by the unicorn to touch my sword to her horn. I stood up and did so. A white light blinded me and filled the room. But, it wasn't just the light that was profound, but the sensation and feeling of a love so pure and powerful that it eclipses human consciousness and understanding. All the entities instantly cleared, and I returned to my physical body.

It was one of the most enchanting experiences I have ever had and just trying to explain it brings tears to my eyes. It is beyond the imagination and human comprehension. Edgar Cayce once said that "What the mind can imagine as possible is real on the astral plane." I will never forget it.

She rescued me despite my rogue and careless attitude. Even when I thought I was alone, I wasn't. Spirit sensed my need for help and sent the unicorn. It's amazing. Life is amazing and magical!

Chapter Thirteen

"Rats I say! Rats!"

Yes, I said, 'rats.' This next experience is rare and highly unusual. The circumstances were unique and most practitioners, if any, will never come across a situation like this one. In all these years, it has only happened to me once. It takes an experienced entity to create such an imaginative and effective scenario. The entity needed the skill and experience to disrupt my dream and convince my consciousness that something else was real, if only temporarily. Most entity clearings are easy and less dramatic than this example.

My husband and I went on a Caribbean cruise. It was our very first and last cruise. The majority of people will go on a cruise with no trouble and have a great time. A cruise is a fantastic vacation and my experience is my own and is a result of the spiritual gifts that I work with. It has nothing to do with cruise ships in general. Actually, this happens to me a lot. When I travel, I am often placed in situations or places that need healing. A person cannot escape his or her destiny. We take ourselves with us where ever we go. Given this aspect of my life and work, they placed me on the one cruise ship that needed healing work.

After boarding the ship, we went to our room. I noticed that every room had a mirror panel closet set of doors that faced the bed. If all the walls of the rooms were removed, it would create a lengthy passage of mirrors, which are well-known for providing access to spiritual worlds. I noticed and disliked this cosmetic foe par right away, but there was nothing I could do about it, so I put it out of my mind.

That night I went to sleep and experienced stressful dreams, but I blamed it on the emotional stress caused by traveling. Still, I instinctually decided not to drink on the cruise. There wasn't any particular reason; I just knew that I shouldn't. A few times, I overheard fellow passengers complain about having bad dreams while they slept. I assumed this was due to the increase in alcohol consumption, and again, I wasn't overly concerned.

I spent the day soaking in the pool, eating great food, enjoying the beautiful ocean views, taking a yoga class and walking under the stars on the top deck. I was in a sublime state and didn't have a care in the world. I went to bed as usual and began dreaming.

Suddenly, I was in a wooden box filled with live rats that were biting me. My first thought was, 'Ouch! This hurts!' My second thought was, 'There's an entity here messing with me.' I didn't experience any fear. At this point in my work, I have seen it all. It caught me off guard since I was in vacation mode and not focusing on work. Once I got over the shock, I pulled my consciousness/spirit body out of the dream scenario created by the entity and reunited with my physical body.

What benefits does any entity receive from this kind of behavior? They merge consciousness and create a connection to the person or dreamer's mind. This allows them to experience the emotion or energy generated by the person's response to the experience. In many ways, it's a form of entertainment for them and a way for a very lonely being to connect with someone or something.

The same method previously discussed was used to clear the entity after I connected with the Divine. I concluded that I had successfully cleared the entity I was sent to clear so I could enjoy the remainder of the cruise. I was happy, but I still didn't drink any alcohol. It just didn't feel right to do so. Alcohol has a weakening effect on the energy field or aura. It can open a person's energy up, making him or her more vulnerable to picking up negative energy from others. It's wise to only drink in a positive, safe environment or at home for this reason. Empaths or sensitive people are more at risk than the general population.

I put on my metaphorical rose-colored glasses and naively went about my day. After a busy day on the cruise, I went to bed expecting a good night's sleep. I entered my dream state as usual and my dream was typical, nothing stressful or weird.

Then everything changed. I found myself in a jungle like setting. I saw men with machine guns holding three prisoners. They were taking turns torturing these men. I hate torture of any kind to man, woman, child, or animal. My point is that I didn't generate this torture scenario from my consciousness. Over the years, I have seen entities use bad dreams to provoke powerful reactions in the dreamer. It took me a minute to figure out what was happening and pull my focus from the torture scene to why I was there. Instead of allowing the dream to distract me with emotion, I focused on the cause of the dream. As soon as I collected my thoughts, I realized another entity must be on the ship. I turned away from the scene and focused on my physical body, and pulled myself back into the physical realm.

It was still in the middle of the night, late and early, at the same time. I realized that there was more activity on the ship than I had previously concluded, so I assessed the environment and the spiritual energy in the space instead of ignoring it because I was on vacation, and I didn't really want to work. (These days, my best vacations are the stay home vacations where the energy is pristine and I can really relax). Ultimately, I yielded to the situation and became involved in the healing process.

I went into meditation and connected with my angel guides. We discussed the situation, and they showed me the entity activity on the ship. It was much more than I realized for several reasons. The mirrors in each room were just one minor component. Of course, the ship was sailing on the ocean. Water is a big conductor of spiritual energy. As I was processing this information with the angels, I thought, 'dah, of course.' The ship contained five large pools of water and several hot tubs. Water was everywhere.

The people didn't help the situation. Many were under emotional stress and consuming large amounts of alcohol, increasing their vulnerability to entity activity. In addition, the crew was a mix of several nationalities and many of the places they came from were dangerous, sad places and a job on a cruise ship was a nice way to escape their living situation. Basically, many people were experiencing emotional struggle in their own way. Some entities were attached to the ship and went where it went, and while others were attached to the people and came on board with them.

I found myself smack dab in the middle of the most entity activity, in one place, than I have previously encountered. This information was overwhelming to me. I didn't know where to start or even if I should.

I voiced my concerns to my angel guides, and they let me know I could use the spiritual amplification power of the water element just like the entities, which combined with their help would give me the boost in energy to do a mass clearing at once. I didn't even know this was possible; however, I was willing to try. I didn't want to continue to stay on the ship with this amount of negative energy on board and since getting off wasn't an option; I needed to do something.

I took some time to center and relax. Over the years, I have learned a lot about entity clearings. I reconnected with my angel guides and followed their instructions for this clearing was going to be a little different.

I called to me all the healing energies such as Reiki and Urevia, along with my spirit guides, animal totems, angels, and the over-souls that were connected to the entities. I let myself drift into a deep meditation on the verge of sleep, but still awake. I took my time, which is very important. If a practitioner rushes, they risk compromising the volume of high vibrational energy they can harness, and then, therefore, do a sloppy job.

After some time passed, and I felt ready; I left my physical body and traveling with my astral body merged my energy with the angels. Together, we drifted above the ship and I noticed my astral body expand in size. I was very large and so were the angels. We were taller and brighter. We created a circle above the ship and, using focused intent and altruistic love, also known as Divine love, which is beyond the human expression of conditional love, we merged all of our energies along with the amplification power of the ocean's energy.

A very large, bright, piercing, golden white light formed in the center of our circle. I began reciting my clearing prayers and opened my heart chakra as large as possible. Beams of light shot out from the center light, connecting with the heart chakras of every entity on board. As the angels and I continued the energy and prayer, the beams of light carried dozens of entities into the center and from there to the soul realm where some just transmuted while others were reunited with their Divine-self after a time of transition.

This clearing process went on for some time, and looking back, I cannot remember how long, but when it was over, the white light in the center of the circle dimmed along with the intensity of the energy flowing through everyone. With love and gratitude, I disconnected from the angels and saw myself shrink down in size and drift back to my physical body.

The night was gone, so I didn't go back to bed. I watched the sun rise and wondered about the effectiveness of the clearing. This was the first time that I took part in a mass clearing of this size. I have experienced the clearing of small groups, of entities, but never this many at once. I needed to wait and see. The results would let me know if the angels and I accomplished our goal.

I had another great day on the cruise, and I went to bed as usual, and I experienced a beautiful sleep. My dreams were normal, and I wasn't bothered by any other energy. Still, I didn't assume everything was perfect. I like to wait at least three nights before I know for sure. It thrilled me to sleep wonderfully the rest of the cruise to the sound of the ocean just outside my balcony.

Going on the cruise taught me that under the right conditions, with the right amplification and support, a mass clearing could be accomplished. However, I am not interested in going on another cruise anytime soon. Although I'm sure it was inspired by a higher power.

Chapter Fourteen

Rescued by a Black Panther

This one isn't exactly a clearing. It is, however, a touching and magical experience I had with spirit. Sometimes when I sleep, my spirit travels to people or places of need. I am a healer by nature, so even in my sleep, I am a healer. Most of the time, this is no big deal. I offer help and go back to my dream state with no issues.

I am grateful and lucky to have a black panther as an animal totem. I call her Peace; though I am sure her real name is far more complicated. She is larger than her earthly counter-parts and her head is as large as a basketball. I love her head. I often rest my forehead on hers and just breathe with my eyes closed. She is the full definition of quiet power and kindness. I am blessed to know her.

In my dreaming state, I went to a place of lower vibration in the astral plane. I found myself in an old abandoned, run-down mansion or maybe an old, large farmhouse. It was larger than the common home, but it wasn't a corporate building or hotel. The rooms had high ceilings and tall doors. I remember a dim, dull green light and everything, even the walls looking dirty and grey.

My intuitive instinct shifted my consciousness from dreaming to being consciously aware of the dream, which is also known as lucid dreaming. I thought to myself that I should go back to my physical body and wake up. I knew that the place was full of negative energy. The colors and shadows were dull and I could feel the weight of the negativity. The smart thing for me to do was to wake up.

I wondered why I had come to this place on this low tier of the astral plane. I decided to look around for just a bit, since I had no intention of staying for a long time or exploring the entire place. I figured I could quickly slip in and be gone before anyone noticed. Yeah, right!

Was I that lucky? You already know the answer as you are reading these words: Nope, I wasn't that lucky. I walked into what looked like a bedroom. Again, everything was saturated with this dull, olive green light. I saw one queen-size bed and a dresser in the room. Before I could turn and leave the room, a female presence jumped from the wall and clung to my back. She had been hiding toward the ceiling at the very top of the wall and I didn't see her.

She wrapped her legs around my waist and her arms around my shoulders and head. I tried to dislodge her by twisting and turning. She wouldn't let go, and I was so lost in thought I forgot where I was and that I could simply wake up. Through practice, a dreamer can acquire the skill to consciously return to his or her physical body at will. I was so concentrated on trying to release myself that I totally forgot.

I am stumbling around, completely forgetting my skills and out of nowhere, the black panther I call Peace appears. She enters the space out of thin air in one giant leap. Peace growled menacingly at the entity and swiped a giant paw as a warning. This scares the entity, and she leaps off my back and returns to her position next to the wall towards the ceiling.

Peace strides around me in a half circle, forming a barrier between me and the entity. She snarls at the entity again and circles me until she is right in front of me. She sits down and looks at me with exasperation. This immediately makes me smile, and she responds to my humor by rolling her eyes back and giving me a look like a mother gives to her child when they do something stupid or reckless. I offer my right hand, palm up, to her, and she places her massive paw on top of my hand. Instantly, her touch returns me back to my physical body.

I don't know how she knew I was in trouble. I didn't call to her. I couldn't think clearly, as I was so preoccupied by the entity on my back. She must have sensed it through our connection. Our angels always know when we need help even though they are not sitting around watching our every moment. There is a heart to heart, spirit to spirit telepathic connection between us and our spirit guides and our loved ones. Information flows back and forth through this connection, even if they are not in the same room with us.

I will treasure this memory. It was magical to me and I am so grateful that Peace blesses me with her presence. I have been good. I haven't wandered into any abandoned, haunted houses on the astral plane since.

Chapter Fifteen

The Impostor

It was the mid-1990's, and I was working hard writing my first set of Urevia Healing Practitioner manuals and helping my husband, run our metaphysical store in addition to teaching healing classes and keeping up with my one-on-one healing practice. Oh, and did I mention planning for our wedding? It was a busy time, to say the least.

I had so much going on that I worked out problems even in my sleep, which isn't uncommon when anyone is in a creative process. I often dreamed about Urevia and how to share the information in such a way that was easy to understand and incorporate. My angels would often assist me at night by giving me information. I spent my day attending to my daily responsibilities. In the tranquility of night, it was easier to hear divine counsel.

After falling asleep, I began to dream. In my dream, I was at the metaphysical store and healing center. In the office I was sitting at my computer, and I was dreaming of writing a section in an Urevia manual. I remember it was a pleasant dream and the light in the room was really bright.

I was absorbed in my work on the computer, with ideas flowing quickly through me. Writing, I was in the midst of a sentence, trying to keep up with the information, when I heard a knock on the door. I turned and saw my mother.

I was so surprised. "Ma, I said, what are you doing here?' She said that she wanted to see me. I stood up and walked towards her, and that's when I felt it: something was off. I paused in front of her and really looked at her. She looked like my mother. Everything was in its place except for the eyes. A certain energy radiates from my mother's brown eyes. The eyes I was looking into were more intense. The color swirled slightly, and there wasn't any love energy in them.

I instantly knew this wasn't my mother, but I didn't let the entity know the jig was up. Instead, I tightly embraced her and held on. I opened my heart chakra and white light began to flow and expand.

The entity realized I had figured it out and tried to break the embrace. I held on to her tighter until the white light expanded and saturated the space, the entity, and me. After a few moments, I returned to my physical body.

This experience isn't particularly interesting except for one thing: entities can take on the appearance of anyone or anything. It is something to keep in mind. I have seen entities take on the form of an animal, a demon, a ghost, something scary, a young child, a person in need, people I know like my husband and, most recently, my brother.

How can we identify an impostor? I will admit that it takes a little practice, but in general, listen to your instincts. Are you confused by the interaction or by what they are saying? Do they feel different? Is the reason for the visit unusual? If in doubt, look carefully at the eyes. If you see anything unusual, disconnect. If it really is a loved one, he or she will understand.

Certain entities are extremely skilled in controlling us and they use our intimate relationships, such as our family and friends, and our emotions, to their advantage. Still, most entities are not sophisticated enough to keep up any illusion long-term. Remember, that they are just pieces of the shadow left behind that have not integrated back into the over-soul as of yet.

On a side note: I want to mention my cat Luna. Generally speaking, dogs help to protect our physical space and cats help to protect our spiritual space. The most recent encounter I had with an impostor was one that took the form of my brother. I was at the kitchen sink doing dishes and when I turned around; I saw my brother. Immediately, I was confused. It was unlike my brother to approach me in the dream state. He and I talk often and if either of us needs something, we address it.

I inquired if he was alright. His answer was vague and confusing. I don't even remember the exact words as I am writing, but I can recall Luna. I heard her cry out first. I angled my head slightly, so that I could get a better view of her and she was sitting on top of the stairway post, pawing the air towards my brother. I couldn't believe it, she was only 7 months old and she was already warning me.

When I saw her, I knew I was dealing with an impostor. My cats over the years will only intervene in my work if something's wrong or to offer help. At this point in my experience, I am aware of the distinction. She was warning me about this entity in my kitchen.

I woke myself up and gave it a couple of days to make sure. I checked in on my brother, and he was fine. When the time was right, I went back in time, because I knew exactly when and where the entity would be, and I crossed him over to the soul plane.

Chapter Sixteen

Instincts

If this kind of work chooses a practitioner, overtime, with experience, he or she will develop finely tuned instincts. So much so that he or she will sense or see an entity as soon as it enters the space, even when sleeping. This gives the practitioner the advantage; enabling him or her to stop an encounter before it begins. As entities are naturally evasive, predicting where and when they will be is the most difficult part of the clearing process.

I was experiencing a good night's sleep drifting in and out of dreams with no stress or concerns. Suddenly, my consciousness stopped all wanderings, and I found myself in my bedroom, but I wasn't in my physical body. That part of me was still resting in the bed.

I heard steps on the stairs leading up to my bedroom. Looking, I saw a hooded, cloaked figure dressed in black with a belt around his or her waist. I wasn't sure if this entity was male or female. I did notice how real it appeared. It wasn't a wisp of energy or something that I could see through. The entity was very solid and was stalking up the stairs towards my resting body.

Now, I know an entity cannot kill me, but I wasn't going to wait around and let it enter my dream state and manipulate my consciousness for its agenda. I zoomed back into my physical body, waking up right before the entity reached me.

I knew the entity would just hang around and wait until I went back to sleep, so I pretended to do just that and went into a meditative state instead. Gathering my energy and connecting with the Divine, I traveled back in time and we cleared the entity at the moment it was on the stairs heading towards my room, and that was that. I never saw it again.

What I find most interesting about this encounter is my aura or energy sensed the presences of the entity, even while sleeping, long before my consciousness. I have gone through so many clearings that even without conscious intent, my energy field and instincts have become attuned to any changes in the electromagnetic fields around me. My subconscious is aware of any shift in the surrounding frequencies.

I have developed an internal alarm system without even trying to do so. I will sometimes wake up in the middle of the night, and I cannot go back to sleep. My subconscious, my body, my energy field is sensing a change in the energy around me and until I resolve it, my subconscious will not allow my conscious mind to fall back to sleep and rest.

Now, I know for some people, waking up in the middle of the night is common and there isn't any presence around them. For those people, your instincts would manifest in different forms of communication or signals to your consciousness to alert you of a possible spiritual presence. But for me, I love to sleep, and sleep comes easily to me. A disruption in my sleep isn't normal. Maybe I'm feeling stressed, the angels trying to tell me something about my work, or a spiritual entity nearby.

Everyone has instincts. It is helpful to pay attention and observe patterns in our behavior, feelings, and energy. Our instincts are an essential part of our intuition, but they are beyond rational thought. Instincts are more like a knowing. This feeling will usually occur abruptly, without any logical cause. I refer to this as 'intuitive instinct.'

Intuitive instinct comes from the sub and super-consciousness. The conscious mind is often distracted by thoughts of the past, present, or future and isn't paying much attention to the surrounding energy. Our intuitive instinct, also known as our animal instinct, is aware of what is happening in our environment. We tend to overlook the guidance because it doesn't follow logical reasoning and uses feelings instead of facts to communicate.

Remember that instinctual signals communicate through the nervous system, as previously discussed. For example, I cannot go back to sleep when there is an energetic disturbance in my space. Everyone is unique, and it is up to the individual to learn the language of his or her instinctual signals.

Chapter Seventeen

Entity Clearing During and After a Healing Session

Entities are usually more active at night, or maybe we are more aware of them at night because our day slows down and we are less distracted. They are still around us during the day, but our consciousness focuses on the physical plane, which gives the entities less access to our mind and emotions. In addition, we travel on the astral/spiritual planes at night when we sleep. When we enter the spiritual planes, especially the lower levels, we are easily accessible to other spiritual beings.

Healings are an exception to the norm. During a healing session, for lack of a better word, a bridge forms between the spiritual planes and the physical plane facilitated by the healing practitioner and healing angel guides. This gives the practitioner greater awareness and access to entity activity.

During a healing session, the client's aura releases stress and lower vibrational energy. As a result of the healing process, a being may lose their link or connection to the client. A rise in vibration occurs when the client's aura becomes healed, balanced, and rejuvenated. The attachment formed by the entity is broken because its vibration is too low, and a similar vibration is needed to keep the connection stable.

A person full of fear, chronic anxiety, hate, anger, and sorrow lowers the vibration of his or her energy field, creating a vulnerable environment for an entity attachment. Please don't freak out. These emotions would need to be intense, chronic, and exposure to an entity such as in a haunted house is all necessary for it to even be a possibility. Most of the time, this isn't the case.

I was giving a healing session to a client I will call Bob, which is not his real name. Bob is a very intense guy. He runs on his nerves and his body is chronically tense. Relaxation isn't part of his lifestyle and he is out of touch with his emotions, motivation, behavior, and spirit. Bob's nervous system is completely exhausted, and he is extremely unhappy, yet he is reluctant to be honest with himself and make some changes.

I tune into a client's energy as we talk a bit before the healing begins. Bob was sharing why he booked the appointment. While he was talking, I noticed movement to the left of his aura. There wasn't any color that I could detect with my physical eyes, just a faint movement in the air or space beside him.

I have learned over the years not to rush the process and let the energy and the experience flow without trying to guide or control it. When I get out of the way, I have more successful outcomes. I resist the urge to make assumptions and just do my job, which is to be a channel for healing energy and information.

Bob lied down on the healing table and I focus on clearing negative energy, opening and rejuvenating his chakra system, which balances the nervous system, and addressing any healing needs in his aura. If I am meant to clear an entity on the spot, while I am performing a healing, they will guide me to do so. It didn't come up during the session. His aura required all of my focus and greatly needed a healing. Again, I knew that the energy movement I saw before his session was left unresolved, but I do not rush the process. I trust Divine timing in all things.

It usually takes one to three days before an entity exposes itself to me after I have disconnected him or her from the host or client during the healing process. In Bob's case, the entity didn't waste any time observing me; it attacked that very night.

I know that an attack is a possibility after giving a healing session, but I don't wait around in anticipation for it to happen. It's just part of my job and there isn't any drama associated with it. I go to bed as normal.

I was sleeping, but I hadn't entered a specific dream yet. What this means is that my consciousness was fully asleep, but that my astral body hadn't left my physical body yet. Bob's entity attacked my astral body by, of all things, biting my neck. No, it wasn't a vampire. It was just really pissed off at me for disconnecting it. The bite temporarily damaged my astral body, but I later repaired the tear with a few sessions.

When it bit me, my hand came up to touch my neck, the entity stepped back at the motion, and I said, "You son of a bitch!" My astral body sat up as my physical body remained motionless, and I gawked at him. The bite caught me off guard. It's not the usual method they use. Before my emotions could get away from me, I didn't say another word and aligned my astral body with my physical body and returned my consciousness to the physical plane whereby, I cleared the entity.

I didn't let my anger get away from me. To do so would lower my vibration and make the crossing of the entity to the Soul plane more difficult. It's important to mention here that I didn't repress my anger; I just remembered the truth: that this is a lost spiritual-being needing my help regardless of its inappropriate behavior. I make mistakes all the time, and I appreciate the grace that has been extended towards me.

If we want forgiveness and grace bestowed unto us, we must be willing to extend the same good will towards others. I understand that there are degrees of bad behavior, some being worse and intentional, but that doesn't change the truth: any being that is alive comes from the same source as we do and, therefore, its success is our success. Eventually, on our journey, all of us will have to decide between being right or valuing the light within everyone more than being right. It's a hard choice. Trusting the light, the life-force energy to teach and heal things long-term is a big ask. The best we can do is to be honorable in our choices and actions and extend as much good-will as possible.

Since I want to be forgiven for my mistakes when they have caused pain to others, I will extend the same curtesy to this entity. Repressing my anger isn't necessary. When we understand the truth, our anger fades and we are one.

Another client, I will call Sue, scheduled a healing session appointment with me. Once the healing started, I realized she had an attachment. I placed my hands on her feet, relaxed my body as much as I could while standing, and my consciousness or spirit left my physical body and entered my astral body.

I wanted to take the entity by surprised, so first, I went to the angel and spirit guide plane. There, I united with them and moving down from the higher spiritual planes, snuck up behind the entity and crossed him over.

Afterwards, I reunited my astral body with my physical and continued the healing session. They guided me to clear the entity during the session. It was an easy entity to cross over and required little time or energy. I like it when I can clear during the session, but it doesn't always work out that way. I might not fully understand why that is, but I have learned to trust the process. There are things at work beyond my understanding, and I have learned that Divine timing is a real thing not to be pushed around or forced.

Chapter Eighteen

Linda's House Clearing

The variety of house clearing ceremonies is endless. The example I offer here is a good place to begin if a practitioner wants to give house clearing work a try. As a person gains in experience and confidence, he or she will add or subtract from this process and the ceremony will become his or her own. A personal connection to the spiritual representation of a ceremony empowers that ceremony, increasing its effectiveness and longevity.

Linda's house was full of activity, both positive and negative. It took four rounds of clearings for me to crossover all the entities haunting the old Victorian house. To make the situation worse, Linda collected antiques, and she had many. Most were okay, but a few were very negative and two had thought-forms attachment to them in addition to the other entities in the house. Thought-forms are composites of negative energy that have accumulated through the passing of time. They are not entities. Think of them as byproducts of extreme negative thought or emotional trauma.

Linda's son referred her to me. She had several health and emotional issues that were getting worse, and it scared her to sleep at night. As with every case, I start with a healing session. The session allows me to assess the situation and get a feel for what I am walking into. Also, the healing serves a vital purpose by detaching any entities that are attached to the client's energy field.

Linda's case was complicated. She was in a very unhappy marriage, elderly with several health issues, her house needed repair, and she was anxious and depressed. The amount of negative energy around her and generated by her was immense. I needed to take a dualistic approach and give her regular healing sessions while I worked behind the scenes, gradually clearing entities a few at a time.

In the meantime, Linda cleaned and decluttered her house on the physical level. The amount of antiques stifled the energy flow of the house. Plus, the house was ancient, and many families lived in it over the years.

Linda destroyed a few of the antiques that were full of negative energy. She really couldn't sell them or give them away, knowing that she would give the person negative energy. It's sometimes possible to clear an item, but in Linda's case, it was easier to burn the minor items and transmute the negative energy by using fire. She felt an instant improvement by getting rid of the objects in her house that were compromising the positive energy in the home.

Together, we created a to-do list and a wellness plan for her. Achieving balance with Linda was the first step before the rest of the house could be cleared. The owner of any house is the dominating energy of the house. She needed to heal enough to be in a positive mind-set.

Linda was making steady progress and felt some relief for the first time in a long time. Over the course of a few weeks, I cleared several entities. I didn't clear them all at once because, as I was clearing one or two, the rest would hide while I focused on the others. I wasn't in a rush, so I didn't worry about it. There is a divine timing to things. I trust the process.

Linda's house was finally ready to be cleared on the spiritual plane: the energetic level of the house that exists on the astral plane. A house clearing ceremony preforms a large healing on the home, removing any residue negative energy and filling the energy of the space with light, love, and positive intentions.

Linda and I discussed how she wanted to live in her home and how she wanted to feel in her home. She wanted to feel safe, creative, and content. I had her design the ceremonial altar with symbols that represented protection, creativity, and peace along with symbols of the Divine, four elements, and her angel guides. She placed the altar in the center of the home.

I did a walk through the house by myself with a pendulum to get a feel for each room. I used the pendulum to confirm areas of negativity. If all is well, the pendulum will rotate in a clockwise circle. After the walkthrough, I gathered the tools needed for the house clearing: drum, tea candles, sea salt, sage, and blessed holy water.

With the drum, I start just outside the main entrance to the house. I pause here to pray and ask for guidance, empowerment, and assistance. I drum in the four directions over the doorway itself. I walk across the threshold, bringing in the Divine light, and move to the most central area of the house. Again, I pause here and facing the North; I call to the energies and angels of the North, inviting them with the beat of the drum. Moving clockwise, I do the same for each direction. Returning to the center, I pray and invite the Divine to work through me and despite me. This creates a sacred circle of light and protection.

I walk to the basement. Starting in the North and moving clockwise, I beat the drum. I remember to pay attention if the drum changes tone in any location. This tells me if there is a greater volume of negative energy in that area. After I drum, I sage the space before moving to the next level or room.

I follow the drumming with energy work. I again start with the basement and perform negative energy extraction in the room or space. With each room, I use the pendulum to test the space and continue this process until all negative energy is cleared before moving to the next step. Once I receive a positive rotation from the pendulum and my instincts tell me all is well, I seal the space by sprinkling holy water in all six directions while saying a prayer of blessing and protection. I finish by placing a tiny pinch of sea salt in all four corners of each room. I light a tea candle in the room asking that as it burns; it fills the room with the intentions of the homeowner.

Returning to the center of the house where the altar sits, I light the altar candle and say a prayer of intention and general blessing. Facing the North direction, I give thanks to the energies and angels of the North bowing in each direction to show respect and gratitude. I continue the same process, moving in a counterclockwise direction, thanking as I go. This releases the sacred circle.

With my drum, I go to the main entrance of the home and step over the threshold, walking outside. Any remaining old or negative energy flows outside, releasing to the light. I place a thin line of sea salt across the threshold of the door, sealing the house and protecting it from negative energy. A practitioner can also encircle the house with herbs and or sea salt by starting in the North direction moving clockwise all the way around the house. It's a nice touch and only takes a few minutes to do.

Note, if the weather is warm, having all the windows open during the ceremony is very useful in the cleansing process. A practitioner can delegate any of these steps to the home owner such has having him or her light the tea candles in each room, stating his or her intention as they go. If the client lives far away, a practitioner can guide him or her through the house clearing ceremony. Everyone has the ability to cleanse old energy and call in the light.

The healing power of a house clearing can last a longtime. However, the health of the homeowner determines the quality of energy in his or her home. Typically, only one house clearing is needed. If there has been major stress in the homeowner's life, another house clearing is very healing and empowering. Furthermore, if somebody desires to make improvements in their life, a house clearing is an effective way to summon in new energy. Last, if a house is really full of negative energy, a few house clearings every six months will heal layers of negative energy that have accumulated over the centuries.

Chapter Nineteen

Spiritual Understanding

I use the terms angels, spirit guides, and animal totems loosely. They are religious and cultural terms, and as such, they are limiting. These terms are used to describe beings of light that are, in reality, beyond the human mind's understanding. The terms entity, ghost, poltergeist, thought-form are also limiting in their own way. These terms are used to describe different forms of energy found on the spiritual planes of existence. We cannot possibly, fully comprehend the spiritual world around us. We only know the spiritual world exists because we sense the connection between our soul and the spiritual energy within each other and the earth we live on. Too many of us have experienced the spiritual world to deny its existence. However, just because we are open to the possibility that something exists, does not mean we fully understand. It's possible because of our beliefs, we are not capable of understanding the spiritual world.

We are like children in grade school, still learning about our own existence. Unfortunately, we do not incarnate as adults with a fully developed brain. We enter the world as helpless infants, with our brains still in development, and our neurons, thoughts, experiences, and beliefs are all shaped by our parents, continuing the same pattern through generations.

The system is flawed. The conditions limiting our young minds extend forward into adulthood, and in some ways, making us very ignorant about the spiritual world. I will assume that is part of the human experience and opportunity for learning. That doesn't mean I have to like it.

All we can do is keep an open mind, heart, and explore. We can try our best to put some structure and reasoning into what we experience and try to interact with the spiritual world, with integrity and love. We already know that fear and judgment create more fear and judgment, which creates emotional pain long-term. Fear is a useless, destructive energy and we don't need to understand the spiritual word to know that. Every day, we witness the effects of our behavior on each other, and the pain that it causes.

It is possible that we have everything wrong, but we have to start somewhere. We emotionally and mentally project on to each other all the time, and that is interacting with other beings that are on the same plane as ourselves. Imagine the projections we place on the astral/spiritual planes. The obvious issue is that we project our human beliefs, assumptions, conditioning, and structure onto the spirit world, but it's all we have.

As we explore the existence of life-force energy in all its forms, the best we can do is keep our ego and the drama out of the interaction. Each person has his or her own spiritual experiences and, therefore, beliefs about life. We work with what we have and start from there, which is learning with integrity. This book describes some of my spiritual experiences processed through my spiritual awareness. I know that my knowledge isn't perfect and is most likely lacking, but I also know that I am making some progress based on the positive results I have achieved over many years. So, the pathway, the relationship I am developing works for me and I am contributing to the world in a positive way. The rest I will learn as I continue my journey.

Each person has to find his or her own spiritual relationship with the God's energy, also known as life-force energy. The good news is that there is nothing to fear. The God/life-force energy of existence secures and supports every person. Make no assumptions and let the journey unfold the truth little by little.

We need to take our time. There's no need to be rushed; we will all eventually return to spirit where all will be known. In the meantime, live with honor, heal your heart or pain, love your life, and show others you love them too: be a positive force in your own life and in this world. The smallest acts of daily kindness and goodwill transmute and heal negative energy.

Disclaimer:

The book provides information from the author's point of view. It is not a diagnostic tool for medical or psychological diagnosis or treatment. It is recommended that an individual seek a licensed professional for all medical and or psychological treatment, for all ailments.

www.ingramcontent.com/pod-product-compliance
Lightning Source LLC
LaVergne TN
LVHW010623100826
845148LV00014B/3079

* 9 7 8 0 9 7 6 4 8 1 9 6 6 *